diversity,

disunity,

and

campus

community

Melvin C. Terrell, editor

December 1992

**Library of Congress
Cataloging-in-Publication Data**
Diversity, disunity, and campus community / edited by
Melvin C. Terrell. — 1st ed.
    p.   cm.
    Includes bibliographical references (p. 225).
    ISBN 0-931654-19-X : $9.95
1. Intercultural education — United States. 2. Minority
college students — United States. 3. College environment —
United States. 4. Pluralism (Social sciences).   I. Terrell,
Melvin C.
LC1099.3.D58   1992   92-32886
370.19'341–dc20   CIP

Monograph Series Editorial Board 1992-93

Other NASPA Monograph Titles

Working with International Students and Scholars on American Campuses

Puzzles and Pieces in Wonderland: The Promise and Practice of Student Affairs Research

The Role of Student Affairs in Institution-Wide Enrollment Management Strategies

The Invisible Leaders: Student Affairs Mid-Managers

The New Professional: A Resource Guide for New Student Affairs Professionals and Their Supervisors

From Survival to Success: Promoting Minority Student Retention

Student Affairs and Campus Dissent: Reflection of the Past and Challenge for the Future

Alcohol Policies and Procedures on College and University Campuses

Opportunities for Student Development in Two-Year Colleges

Private Dreams, Shared Visions: Student Affairs Work in Small Colleges

Risk Management and the Student Affairs Professional

Contents

Contributors

Melvin C. Terrell, Editor, Vice President for Student Affairs and Associate Professor of Counselor Education, Northeastern Illinois University, Chicago, Illinois

Margaret H. Duggar, Technical Editor, Professor of English, Chicago State University, Chicago, Illinois

Charles Brown, Associate Vice President for Student Affairs and Adjunct Associate Professor of Higher Education Administration, University of Alabama, Tuscaloosa, Alabama

Raymond Dye, Vice President for Student Affairs, San Francisco State University, San Francisco, California

John I. Gilderbloom, School of Urban Policy, University of Louisville, Louisville, Kentucky

Dennis C. Golden, Vice President for Student Affairs, University of Louisville, Louisville, Kentucky

Suzanne Gordon, Associate Vice Chancellor for Student Affairs and Dean of Students, University of Arkansas-Fayetteville, Fayetteville, Arkansas

Victoria L. Guthrie, Assistant Vice President for Student Affairs, Bellarmine College, Louisville, Kentucky

Barbara Henley, Vice President for Student Affairs, Northern Illinois University, Dekalb, Illinois

John R. Hoeppel, Director of Counseling, Northeastern Illinois University, Chicago, Illinois

Marvalene Hughes, Vice President for Student Affairs and Professor of Educational Psychology, University of Minnesota, Minneapolis, Minnesota

Gordon H. Lamb, President, Northeastern Illinois University, Chicago, Illinois

Bruce D. La Vant, Director of Preparatory Division and Adjunct Assistant Professor of Educational and Counseling Psychology, University of Louisville, Louisville, Kentucky

Robbie L. Nayman, Vice President for Student Affairs, California State University, Fullerton, California

Emmanuel Newsome, Vice President for Student Affairs, Florida Atlantic University, Boca Raton, Florida

Lillian Poats, Assistant Professor of Administration and Higher Education, Texas Southern University, Houston, Texas

Theresa Powell, Vice President for Student Affairs, Western Michigan University, Kalamazoo, Michigan

James Renick, Vice Provost, George Mason University, Fairfax, Virginia

Shirley Stennis Williams, Dean of Education, Edinboro University of Pennsylvania, Edinboro, Pennsylvania

Connie Borders Strode, Graduate Assistant, University of Arkansas-Fayetteville, Fayetteville, Arkansas

Doris J. Wright, Associate Professor of Counseling, Georgia State University, Atlanta, Georgia

Foreword

We started hearing the language associated with the challenges of what was then generally called *pluralism* several years ago. The new jargon filtered from academic and political theorists to corporate boardrooms where it surfaced in such phrases as "managing cultural diversity." The message given to management trainees was basically one of benign tolerance of people from backgrounds other than their own. The concept then grew into "understanding cultural diversity," and the thrust became more one of studious appreciation than tolerance, i.e., appreciation in the liberal arts sense of art appreciation or music appreciation. But that wasn't and isn't enough.

Now we, in the academy, have entered an activist phase of coming to grips with a world in which our colleagues, our students, our customers, our neighbors — the people with whom we conduct day-to-day business — are increasingly culturally diverse. The phrase itself has come to encompass more than race; it also recognizes people of various ethnicities, generations, genders, sexual preferences, geographic areas, physical abilities, and even professions.

While the concepts and realities of cultural diversity have evolved over the last three decades, they are no longer futuristic. We are learning cultural diversity, correctly or incorrectly, by living it. Cultural diversity is emerging as both a theoretical and a highly pragmatic discipline in its own right, particularly applicable for professionals in student affairs who set the tone for the campus through attitude, behavior, and programming. This monograph demonstrates how, through our research and experiences, the student affairs subculture can provide academic as well as managerial leadership by building bridges between academic affairs, development, and administrative affairs functions in our institutions to develop a conscious level of planned change.

The pockets of parochialism will shrink, conflicts will be prevented rather than resolved, and we will go beyond diversity based on numbers to diversity based on collaboration. The Ivory Tower will be viewed by our larger communities not as a structure apart from reality but as a vital link to the global, social, and economic structures of the next century.

— Gordon H. Lamb
Northeastern Illinois University

Acknowledgements

During the countless hours I spent preparing the monograph, I developed an appreciation for the contributors' indispensable roles in making *Diversity, Disunity, and Campus Community* a reality. I owe an incalculable debt to Constance Rockingham whose initial encouragement and support convinced me that I was capable of editing a monograph. I thank the NASPA Monograph Series Editorial Board for their unswerving attention to detail that made working with them a pleasure. Special recognition and appreciation go to Margaret Duggar whose contributions as technical editor were essential to the realization of this project.

In addition, I appreciate the assistance provided by my secretarial staff: Linda Leyva and Jasmine N. Walker. Also my assistant, Donna Rudy, helped to refine the project. Finally, I want to thank my parents, Mr. and Mrs. Cleveland Terrell, for their love and deep understanding.

— Melvin C. Terrell
Editor

Overview

Marvalene Hughes

Diversity, Disunity, and Campus Community was chosen as the title of this monograph to portray the paradoxical qualities inherent in pursuing diversity. As universities assume their missions and mandates to provide education for an increasingly heterogeneous student population, it becomes clear that university leaders and practitioners must address diversity by acquiring the necessary skills and visions to create and nurture a campus climate conducive to living and learning for the new student population. Demographically, universities have witnessed profound shifts as more ethnically and racially diverse students; women; disabled students; older students; gay, lesbian, and bisexual students; and international students seek their place in institutions of higher learning. These groups increasingly demand an active and strong voice in policy development, as well as in planning and implementing the process of education. Like becoming an educated citizen, achieving diversity is a process.

The static state which typified curricular and cocurricular education in the past is under siege as proponents of diversity and anti-multicultural demagogues articulate opposing *raisons d'etre*. These dynamic opposing forces forecast and dramatize the challenges societies face in aspiring to become diverse. They are compelling and revealing symbols of a revolution which is confronting the institutional inertia in education in a manner heretofore unparalleled, and creating a state of disequilibrium. Profound change occurs when the static state of higher education is shocked out of complacency by the disequilibrium generated by diversity. What is different about this revolution is that it is not transitory; it is unlikely that society and its institutions can ever return to the traditional static state. Unfortunately, some universities and colleges resort to political expediency by acquiescing to the demands of separatists and isolationists. Unless efforts are made to create and nurture a campus multicultural environment, diversity has not been addressed.

When we embrace multiculturalism, the fabric of our local, national, and global societies will be differently woven. It is reasonable to postulate that our new impetus for multiculturalism signals that we are on the cusp of the paradigm shift. This is not a revisit of the '60s. A poignant manifestation of the shift reveals that diversity and education are as much a process as a product. Hence, as educators, we must concern ourselves with the art (process) and the outcome (product) of education and diversity. There is sufficient evidence that we commit strategic errors when we value orchestration of the process (the art) of achieving diversity over the outcome, or vice versa. In both instances, our focus must be on excellence, and we must accept the premise that we cannot attain excellence without concurrently mastering the competencies to achieve diversity. Like education, diversity must never be reduced to an outcome (product) denominator. The *zietgeist* of process and product characterizes the need for perpetual foci on diversity programming and underscores that diversity requires fluidity, flexibility, and continual attention to human details. Whether or not diversity remains an overt agenda for administrators and practitioners, it will forever be a force influencing decision making either directly or indirectly.

This monograph offers perspectives for higher educators on the process and product of diversity, ranging from the traditional micro, campus-based practices employed today to the introduction of macro-student development, as reflected in global diversity. Caution must be exercised in introducing global diversity, particularly in an environment where domestic diversity has not been adequately addressed. The "limited resources and goods" assumptions which pervade our culture could exacerbate frustrations of marginalized groups as global diversity is introduced.

In Chapter One, Henley, Powell, and Poats focus the reader's attention on the future of cultural diversity. In this chapter, they refer to subsequent chapters and review related studies on the topic of diversity. The authors set the stage for a critique of politics involving some new challenges, including: political correctness, federal roadblocks, free speech, and growing incivility.

Distinction is made between free speech and hate speech, but they acknowledge that precedent has been established for the courts to overturn any ruling which protects individuals from any expressions, including hate expressions. Court rulings, federal roadblocks, and the politically correct movement are presented as counterforces toward achieving diversity. Political winds are blowing in the antidiversity direction, but cultural diversity on campus will ultimately be determined by the administration's commitment to recruiting and retaining a diverse population of students, faculty, and staff. Henley, Powell, and Poats end on a bright note, suggesting that campuses must aspire to be models to our external and internal communities as the world struggles to honor diversity.

Using a survey designed to assess: 1) the extent of campus efforts to promote cultural diversity; 2) institutional characteristics; 3) the administrative structure of respondent institutions, and; 4) background variables of the individual respondents, Terrell and Hoeppel present findings from their survey of 179 NASPA institutional members in Region IV-East. There are clear indications that a high percentage (78 percent) of the institutions surveyed recognize the importance of diversity on campus, and, further, these institutions view their efforts to address this agenda to be action oriented (92 percent reported active programming efforts). Residence hall staff reported a lower level (60 percent) of diversity programming. As expected, most programming efforts are directed toward students (84 percent) with declining foci on administrators (67 percent), faculty (64 percent) and residence hall staff (54 percent). Larger campuses were more attentive to diversity on a day-to-day basis, but neither large nor small institutions had prepared future strategies. Similarly, size of the on-campus residential population was a mitigating factor in determining the importance of diversity. The authors note a lagging tendency on the part of faculty to introduce curricular infusions which could potentially offer opportunities to mainstream diversity. The chapter underscores the continuing practice of institutions to relegate this agenda to students affairs leadership.

Wright tackles the issue of enhancing the campus climate through partnership with campus law enforcement in Chapter Three. Wright offers a historical accounting of the range in roles and attitudes by those charged to enforce law and order on campuses. She acknowledges the disparity which often exists between the "police" training of law enforcement and the expectations of administrators and students that campus officers possess unique sensitivity to the higher education community. She offers the perspective that it is essential that all campus law enforcement officers become student development educators. Wright concludes that campus law enforcement officers are especially important to the diversity mission at a time when hate crime law is under siege, yet campuses seek to increase their diversity through recruitment. Her recommendations include: 1) diversity training programs for officers; 2) increased professionalization of those assigned to higher education; 3) a model for student civilian police training, and; 4) increased alliance between student affairs and law enforcement officers.

How and why institutions create change to achieve diversity is the theme of Chapter Four by Gordon and Strode. Seven of nine institutions contacted agreed to participate in an institutional change analysis. Data were analyzed using Hammond's organizational development model which describes four stages: 1) awareness of the need for change; 2) diagnosis of strengths and weaknesses; 3) planning strategies and follow-up actions; and 4) monitoring, evaluating, and stabilizing. The seven institutions became case studies for researchers who examined mission statements, program materials, and information; and interviewed key participants to ascertain stages of progress toward diversity. Awareness of a need for diversity was either precipitated by enlightened leadership empowered to create change (boards and presidents) or students who mandated change via political activism. Perceptions of change as experienced by presidents and students revealed that progress is measured and slow. Institutions, in the main, are in the stages of awareness program planning. All participants expressed perceptions of gradual progress.

In Chapter Five, Golden, Guthrie, and Gilderbloom summarize the University of Louisville's first university-wide celebration of diversity. This week-long celebration gave the university a "power surge" for the diversity initiative. The authors present a week-long program model and format and discuss outcomes of the Louisville celebration. They report on profound change occurring, including increased student aid, commitment to an annual celebration, increased hiring of minority faculty and staff, strengthened recruitment and retention efforts, commitment to community building, increase in research projects which focus on diversity, and creation of a center for cultural diversity.

As dean of education, Williams is uniquely positioned to present an academic response to campus climate issues. In Chapter Six, she summarizes two initiatives in the University of Wisconsin System — Planning the Future, adopted in 1986, and Wisconsin Design for Diversity, adopted in 1988. Both initiatives were introduced to emphasize the need to address diversity system-wide in Wisconsin. The plan went a step beyond most in that the president warned that diversity must not be viewed as the business of a few specialists; it must become a partnership undertaken by academicians and others in the campus community. To demonstrate the centrality of this mandate in the academic community, a campus-level academic requirement was introduced which broadened educational requirements to include ethnic studies. After surveying 13 senior minority academic professionals in the University of Wisconsin System, Williams offers recommendations to 1) introduce senior faculty mentors; 2) conduct minority faculty and staff conferences; 3) create funded opportunities for minority faculty research; 4) grow your own doctorates; 5) identify special funds to support race and ethnic projects, and; 6) infuse the curriculum with ethnic requirements. Readers are cautioned that even these measures are not a panacea.

Student leaders' perspectives and perceptions of racism on campus may be key to understanding others' views of racism in the campus environment. La Vant, Brown, and Newsome acknowledge the enormous power and influence of student leaders in creating a campus climate conducive to diversity. Student leaders' perceptions of racism may influence the growth and development of their peers in racial awareness and identity development. The authors randomly sampled three major universities to assess student leaders' perceptions of racism. They discovered student leaders perceive racism as prevalent on campus and that it impacts on interracial friendships, dating and socializing. Student leaders are at various levels with their own diversity identity development; their perceptions undoubtedly serve as a filter and, thereby, gauge their effectiveness in situations involving race relations. Student leaders' training programs must prepare them to understand their values, attitudes, and beliefs regarding racism and to apply their skills acquired in training meaningfully as they plan their programs and activities for others in the campus community.

California may be viewed as a laboratory to test the diversity agenda because of its geographical proximity to Mexico, the Pacific Rim migration, and the rapidly growing populations of color within the state. Nayman, Renick, and Dye examine strategies employed by the California State University System to promote access, equity, and diversity. Key legislative mandates served as catalysts to the state universities' actions to address diversity. As the largest and most diverse state university system, California has introduced special support programs similar to those in other universities. The authors surveyed chief student affairs officers in the state university system to establish a profile of existing programs and solicit perceptions of program effectiveness. Chief student affairs officers in the state university system gave programs average ratings of effectiveness. Lack of faculty involvement and lack of coordination were identified as major weaknesses in the system. The authors conclude that public policy has driven the California State University System to organize responsive programs and assess their effectiveness.

In the final chapter on global diversity, I identify nine universal human values and introduce principles of macro-student development. These principles emerged from international research, conducted during the past seven years, involving 34 countries. These universal values are viewed as the key to world view understanding and macro-human development which transcends all forces that divide human beings. It is suggested that internationalization of education is imminent. Therefore, we can and must cultivate it by understanding the importance of global, universal human values and by aspiring to live by these principles wherever we are. A seven-stage model facilitates individual and group assessment of diversity readiness on a continuum. Practical suggestions for leadership are offered.

There are rising expectations that colleges and universities are making progress in their efforts to promote diversity on campus. Forces and counterforces, both internal and external to campuses, can distract leaders, diffuse their resources and energies, and steer them off their established course of action. This monograph summarizes typical problems confronting higher education in pursuit of a diverse campus climate and offers some practical and theoretical perspectives to keep educators on course and influence their future actions.

CHAPTER ONE

Achieving Cultural Diversity
Meeting the Challenges

Barbara Henley
Theresa Powell
Lillian Poats

The importance of cultural diversity as an issue for the nation's colleges and universities is undeniable — this issue has been the subject of considerable discussion. National meetings and conferences have offered sessions on the topic to provide administrators, faculty and staff members, and students an arena for discussion.

The achievement of cultural diversity has become a goal for many colleges and universities. Subsequent chapters in this monograph will delineate the genesis of this goal: a recognition of the growing numbers of African Americans, Hispanics, Native Americans, and Asian Americans in the United States; and the need to address increased racial conflict on the campuses.

Kuh, Schuh, Whitt, Andreas, Lyons, Strange, Krehbiel, and MacKay (1991) noted that ". . . at some institutions which have attracted increasing numbers of students from different racial and ethnic backgrounds, tolerance of differences is not a satisfactory aspiration" (p. 296). We agree that mere tolerance is not adequate. Colleges and universities need to find ways to embrace African American, Hispanic, Native American, and Asian American students in a supportive environment to achieve cultural diversity. It may not be an easy goal to reach because "old habits die hard." Nevertheless, institutions must strive to achieve diversity and be prepared to face many challenges in the process.

CHALLENGES TO ACHIEVING CULTURAL DIVERSITY

The achievement of cultural diversity will be determined by the degree to which colleges and universities are able to address the issues and establish some of the initiatives outlined in this monograph. There will be many challenges encountered which must be met. Strategies need to be developed to meet them. Only by doing so can we be assured of achieving cultural diversity on our campuses in the future. Currently, several major challenges appear to be prevalent: inadequate levels of funding for higher education; recruitment and retention of African Americans, Hispanics, Native Americans, and Asian Americans; the campus climate; and the federal climate.

Funding

Inappropriate levels of funding for higher education continue to be a challenge to achieving cultural diversity. The nationally circulated *Chronicle of Higher Education Almanac* ("The Nation, Institutions," 1991) reported the results of an American Council on Education (ACE) survey of 359 college and university administrators. Eighty-four percent listed financial concerns as the top challenge they will face in the next five years. Many states across the country are already beginning to experience serious financial woes. ACE reported that 21 percent of the senior administrators at the 359 universities surveyed indicated either a decrease or no change in their campus operating budgets from 1989-90 to 1990-91 ("The Nation, Institutions," 1991). In Illinois, higher education received a 1 percent and a 3 percent mid-year budget reduction during the 1990-91 and 1991-92 academic years, respectively. Furthermore, there were no funds appropriated by the state legislature for salary increases for the 1991-92 year. Colleges and universities must have sufficient financial support to direct some of the funds to initiatives designed to achieve cultural diversity.

Recruitment and Retention

Integrally connected to limited financial resources are the issues of recruitment and retention of African Americans, Hispanics, Asian Americans, and Native Americans whose participation in higher education is essential to achieving cultural diversity. Casualties of shrinking financial resources "have been the 'nonessentials'– special services, ethnic studies, women's centers, and other special population programs" (Wright, Butler, Switzer & Masters, 1988, p. 99), including recruitment efforts. While African Americans, Hispanics, and Native Americans showed gains in enrollment in higher education between 1986 and 1988, their persistence and degree attainment rates were lower than Caucasian and Asian American students (Carter & Wilson, 1991). Students from underrepresented racial groups must be retained to achieve diversity.

Campus Climate

Another challenge to achieving cultural diversity is the campus climate. If one uses demographic projections alone, it appears that cultural diversity should be achieved automatically on campuses, since it is projected there will be an increase in the number of African American, Hispanic, and Asian American students. However, an influx of large numbers of these students will not ensure a culturally diverse campus which depends not only on the increased numbers but also on the campus' receptivity and responsiveness to the students and their needs.

Campuses are laden with several distressing environmental issues: racial tensions and violence; the perception of hostility as a result of acts of incivility; the lack of culturally enriching activities and/or cultural awareness; feelings of personal isolation and the perception of insensitivity to the needs of underrepresented groups; the lack of faculty involvement as role models and mentors with African American, Hispanic, Native American, and Asian American students; and accusations of "political correctness." College campuses are becoming powder kegs which are about to explode. Cultural diversity cannot be achieved nor can it thrive in such environments.

The proliferation of racial incidents has been discussed in several sources (Farrell, 1988; Henley, 1990; Louis, 1987). In addition, negative feelings about affirmative action and support programs for differently prepared students, cultural misunderstandings, and competition for scarce resources have contributed to the escalation of hostility toward African American, Hispanic, Native American, and Asian American students. Universities must address the issue of racism and the increase in feelings of hostility if cultural diversity is to be achieved.

The lack of culturally enriching activities and/or cultural awareness has also contributed to a negative campus climate. An idea central to cultural diversity is that individuals should experience and take pride in their own cultural background. The notion of a melting pot is challenged as each underrepresented group struggles to maintain certain aspects of their culture while integrating into mainstream America. This is evidenced on college campuses by the student requests for activities which highlight various cultures. African American, Hispanic, Native American, and Asian American students tend to respond positively to activities planned for them and to opportunities to have appropriate input into the activities offered, especially those which reflect their cultural experiences (Henley, 1990). Administrators, faculty members, and students must be mindful of the value of culturally diverse programs and activities.

Feelings of isolation have often been reported by students from underrepresented groups matriculating at predominantly white institutions (Lomotey, 1990). The paucity of these students on campus is often one of the first things a new African American, Hispanic, Asian American, or Native American student will notice. This paucity confirms to the student ". . . that the university was not built for them and that they do not belong" (Saufley, Cowan & Blake, 1983, p. 5). Farrell and Jones (1988) cited isolation as a serious problem and suggested that it was the result of increased racial discrimination on college campuses. We need to help students overcome feelings of isolation if the campus climate is to be improved.

Another campus climate issue is the perception that administrators, faculty, staff, and the campus, in general, are insensitive to the needs of African American, Hispanic, Native American, and Asian American students. Many institutions have implemented programs and activities designed to address the students' needs. Chapter Four provides a review of such programmatic thrusts and reveals that some have been extremely effective, while others have done little to impact the recruitment and/or retention of minority students on campus. A key ingredient in successful programs has been the involvement of individuals who are caring and sensitive to the needs of the students. Gunnings (1982) found that minority students often expected minority administrators to serve as role models, surrogate parents, and advocates on predominantly white campuses. However, minority faculty, administrators, and staff are not the only ones who are responsible for creating a caring environment that is responsive to the needs of the students.

The lack of faculty involvement with minority students as role models, mentors, or caring individuals has contributed to a negative campus climate. Positive interaction with faculty members can enhance the probability of success for students from underrepresented racial groups. Allen (1988) stated that many African American students felt awkward with majority faculty and this was a problem in higher education. He recommended that institutions involve faculty more extensively in recruiting and retaining African American students. There are countless instances where institutions developed programs to address the needs of African American students without faculty involvement. The lack of faculty involvement or the presence of faculty resistance to the programs meant that students returned, in many instances, to classrooms with uncaring, insensitive individuals. It is imperative that faculty involvement be a major component of any effort to address campus climate issues. After all, students spend a large part of their campus life in classrooms with the faculty.

Accusations of "political correctness" (PC), another issue which can threaten the achievement of a positive climate, abound on many campuses. Current efforts to address the climate have been labeled by some as attempts to stifle free speech and academic freedom, close debate, police thoughts, change the Eurocentric curriculum, censor campus publications, and force more affirmative action faculty and staff hirings and student admissions. Efforts to make the campus more comfortable socially and academically for underrepresented groups have resulted in charges of PC and have spawned the PC movement.

Reactions to the PC term have resulted in the drawing of battle lines in academia. Individuals who are committed to improving the campus climate and valuing and achieving diversity have been charged with intolerance of persons and opinions differing from their own (Abudu, 1991). Charges against many of these individuals are being led by the National Association of Scholars (NAS) which expressed its opposition to affirmative action, sensitivity workshops, multicultural studies, and race-targeted scholarships (Conciatore, 1991).

It appears that NAS wants to maintain the status quo in academia. Perhaps its members have no problem with the decline in the enrollment and graduation rates of African American students, the campus racism, and the "chilly" environment for members of the underrepresented groups. However, a strongly negative environment can inhibit a student's ability to receive an education (Delgado, 1991; Henley, 1991).

Teachers for a Democratic Culture, a new organization founded primarily by English professors, has emerged to counter the arguments and positions taken by NAS. This new organization of scholars expressed a commitment to improving the campus climate and to valuing and achieving diversity especially in their efforts to expand the undergraduate curriculum (Heller, 1991). Ostensibly, members of the new organization have made a deliberate decision not to sit by idly and allow another group to promote an agenda antithetical to cultural diversity.

The Federal Climate
In the 1980s, the term *Reaganomics* was coined to refer to budgetary cuts in educational and social programs made by then-President Ronald Reagan. The term *Bushwhacking* may be the appropriate term for the 1990s to describe the actions by President George Bush and his administration that undercut efforts to achieve cultural diversity. For two years, President Bush denounced civil rights legislation proposed by members of the U.S. Congress as a "quota bill" which specified the numbers of "minorities" who should be hired and promoted (American Council on Education, 1991). Some members of Congress stated that the bill was not a "quota bill" but contained the same language as the Americans with Disabilities Act signed by President Bush in 1990. If this were true, why did he denounce the bill? The

bill was eventually signed in 1991 after David Duke, an ex-Ku Klux Klansman who claimed to be a member of the President's political party, participated in a runoff election for the governorship of Louisiana, and "it suddenly became important for the White House to stop playing on racial fears and adopt a tone of moderation" ("A Turnabout," 1991).

During a commencement address at the University of Michigan in 1991, President Bush decried perceived attempts on campuses to stifle debate and abridge individuals' rights to freedom of speech (Cockburn, 1991). Since all speech is not protected currently, President Bush's "Michigan Address" was viewed as an insult to the members of university communities who were attempting to establish or preserve some semblance of civility and more positive environments on campuses for all students. The address may also be remembered for the site that was chosen. We wonder why the speech was made at the University of Michigan which was rocked by much diversity conflict and whose first speech code was overturned by the court on the grounds that it had a "chilling" effect on the educational process. What about the "chilling" effect of racial and sexual harassment on the ability of African Americans, Hispanics, Asian Americans, and Native Americans to receive an education?

Michael Williams, the assistant secretary for civil rights in the U.S. Department of Education, pronounced the illegality of minority scholarships in December 1990. This created more confusion and controversy around the issue of cultural diversity and sent shock waves throughout academic circles where attempts to increase access to higher education were in progress (Abudu, 1991). Although Lamar Alexander, secretary of the U.S. Department of Education and a President Bush appointee, disavowed Michael Williams' pronouncement, race-targeted scholarship programs were

subjected to a review under his leadership (Abudu, 1991).
New regulations have now been proposed "that generally
would bar colleges from setting up scholarships reserved for
members of specific ethnic or racial groups" (Jaschik, 1991).
We await the final ruling on this additional threat to diversity
by the federal government.

Secretary Alexander has waged yet another battle against
diversity. As a member of the Bush administration, he
expressed his opposition to diversity as a Middle States
Association accreditation standard (Abudu, 1991). He
deferred the renewal of the "accrediting agency's recognition
pending further study of diversity standards [which] he
[suggested were] potentially antithetical to academic freedom
and institutional autonomy, and potentially in violation of
federal civil rights laws by leading to what he [feared] as the
imposition of race-based hiring quotas" (Abudu, 1991, p. 48).

If cultural diversity is to be achieved on campuses, this
nation's leaders must examine the impact of their decisions
which appear to be unsupportive of efforts to diversify.
College and university faculty, staff, administrators, and
students who want to achieve cultural diversity also must
make their voices heard across the nation and in the nation's
capital.

There are many challenges confronting the achievement
of cultural diversity at our colleges and universities. Meeting
the challenges will not be easy. It is imperative that we
develop effective strategies to meet these challenges and to
ensure the full participation of African Americans, Hispanics,
Native Americans, and Asian Americans in American higher
education.

STRATEGIES FOR MEETING
THE CHALLENGES

The future of cultural diversity on the campus depends on how well we are able to address the previously discussed major challenges: funding; recruitment and retention of underrepresented groups; the campus climate, and the federal climate.

Funding

In light of declining state and federal support, colleges and universities must pursue new funding sources to achieve cultural diversity. Business and industry have come to realize their vested interest in supporting education and preparation of their work force for the future. Partnerships with business and industry will need to be developed or strengthened. Wright et al. (1988) listed endless possibilities for partnerships:

> One strategy might be to interest business in adopting higher education support activities such as student affairs programs, student union campus programming, or the counseling center because (good selling point) they are needed and therefore appreciated by all students — which warms the heart of every public relations person (p. 110).

Recruitment

All members of the admissions staff will need to make special efforts to recruit students from diverse racial backgrounds. In addition, current students, faculty and staff members, and alumni from underrepresented groups can be involved formally in the recruitment process. It will be necessary for members of colleges and universities to interact with potential students earlier in the educational pipeline. An adopt-a-school program should be established to help prepare students for higher education. This would be a powerful recruitment tool. Other recruitment tools include established community institutions such as churches and community agencies, and attractive television and radio advertisement campaigns. These media, especially, continue to hold great appeal to young people.

Recruiters must learn how to recruit not just the potential student but the entire family whose influence on college choices for Hispanics and African Americans is great. Athletic recruiters have developed some strategies in this area that we need to adapt. For example, visitation programs which enable prospective students and their parents to visit the campus should be used to attract the student and the family.

Retention
The successful recruitment alone of African Americans, Hispanics, and other underrepresented groups will not ensure the achievement of cultural diversity. Wright et al. (1988) suggested several social, economic, and environmental conditions for the successful retention of minority students:

❑ Racism, sexism, and other forms of bias must be controlled or managed

❏ The social climate must encourage open, flexible interactions among all members of the campus community, from maintenance to personnel to administration

❏ Student enrollment must reflect and respect ethnic diversity

❏ Institutions must employ culturally skilled and technically competent professional staff/faculty

❏ Developmental/instructional support programs should exist to supplement students' classroom instruction with culture-specific learning tools

❏ Institutions' historical relationships with minority communities should be understood and, where those interactions are poor, actively enhanced

❏ Retention programs and services should be funded aggressively with emphasis placed on securing permanent institutional financial support (p. 101).

It is not enough to establish a program, place it in a corner, and expect only the faculty and staff assigned to it to be responsible for retention. Successful efforts depend on the cooperation and commitment of individuals at all levels of the university. Retention is everyone's responsibility and must be addressed to achieve cultural diversity.

Campus Climate

Because the climate on many campuses poses a unique challenge to achieving cultural diversity, we must address the issues which contribute to inhospitable campus environments.

The first issue is the proliferation of racism on college campuses. Some campuses have made positive attempts to address racism. Several chapters in this volume and the research literature highlight some of the efforts: the appointment of response teams; seminars; sensitivity and prejudice reduction workshops; regional and national conferences; celebrations of diversity, the hiring of a more diverse faculty, staff and administration; the recruitment of more diverse students; required multicultural courses, curriculum revisions to include non-Western ideas; discrimination hot lines; peer interventions; the establishment of multicultural centers; new student orientation programs; unity rallies; research; and the adoption of university discrimination action plans, to name a few. These efforts must continue.

Concomitantly, racial incidents and all forms of harassment must be condemned in the strongest possible language by the faculty, staff, students, and administration. This condemnation will help to establish and support a community standard of respect for all members. Proactive and reactive efforts to quell racial unrest and discrimination will need to be intensified if cultural diversity is to be achieved.

A second issue is the growing perception of hostility and incivility on campuses. Although there are many convincing arguments against antiharassment and restrictive speech codes, members of groups which have been victimized historically may need some form of protection. There are laws against sexual harassment. Campuses have sexual harassment policies which are distributed widely on campuses. Why are not there racial harassment policies which receive the same wide distribution? Do not African Americans and Hispanics deserve to study in environments, which are their workplaces, free of harassment? Colleges have been urged to enact appropriate policies. The Illinois Bar Association adviscd colleges to adopt antiharassment policies which banned deliberate action or the creation of a hostile environment (Flaherty, 1991). Achieving cultural diversity may depend, in part, on the ability of a college or university to afford students some degree of protection from harassment.

The lack of culturally enriching activities, the feelings of isolation, the perceptions of insensitivity to the needs of underrepresented groups, and the lack of faculty involvement as role models or mentors are also issues which must be addressed. Student organizations and other university-sponsored activities must be offered for African American, Hispanic, Native American, and Asian American students. These students need to have input in the programming efforts. They also need a deliberate and specific invitation to participate in mainstream activities. Mentoring programs which involve peers, faculty, staff members, and community leaders as mentors need to be established (O'Brien, 1988). Forums to address myths, stereotypes, and backlashes need to be provided. The successful recruitment of more students, faculty and staff members, and administrators from underrepresented groups will help address these issues.

Another issue is the "political correctness" movement. Individuals who are committed to valuing and achieving cultural diversity may be accused continually of attempting to impose a correct political agenda on campuses. Those individuals need to articulate vociferously the consequences for the nation if any segment of the population is not educated.

Mere access will not ensure a college education. A more balanced curriculum; the hiring of a more diverse faculty, staff, and administration; the recruitment of more diverse students; advocacy of antiharassment codes; and a continued resolve to create a more supportive and hospitable environment for African Americans, Hispanics, Asian Americans, and Native Americans are essential to achieving cultural diversity.

The Federal Climate
A final issue that must be addressed involves the roadblocks erected by our national leadership. Either through direct appeal or at ballot boxes during elections, members of the current administration need to be lobbied to provide the political and moral leadership for valuing and achieving cultural diversity in the nation and throughout all of this nation's institutions. The lobbying efforts should focus primarily on maintaining scholarships that will ensure access for African Americans and Hispanics and on increased federal funding for education.

A campus' success in meeting the many challenges to achieving cultural diversity will depend on leadership from the top. However, individuals at all levels of the institution, not just student affairs professionals, must play a role in achieving cultural diversity. Governing boards, presidents, administrators, faculty and staff members, and students must contribute to the efforts. The future of the country and the future of the university will depend on our doing so.

Because the Caucasian population will not increase at the same accelerated rate as African Americans and Hispanics, members of the latter groups will have to fill many seats at universities and colleges to maintain enrollments at reasonable levels. Heterogenous, supportive, and hospitable environments will be needed to attract and retain these groups. McCauley (1988) found that African American students will leave a predominantly white campus because of its homogeneity. Moreover, the enrollment of African American students at historically African American colleges has increased due, in part, to the inhospitable environments on many predominantly white campuses ("Blacks' College Pick," 1990). Historically African American colleges are unable to admit all of the African American students who apply because these colleges do not have enough seats or resources.

In addition, it would be a devastating blow if predominantly white universities lost the opportunity to educate these students. Significant enrollment declines would have serious economic consequences for individual members of the academy, the institution, the community or town, and the nation. Furthermore, the campus would be void of the cultural enrichment it could enjoy with the presence of underrepresented groups. Therefore, it is in everyone's self-interest to be committed to achieving cultural diversity.

AN AGENDA FOR CHANGE

The challenges delineated above are not an exhaustive list. There are and there will be other challenges. We offer several agenda items which consist of strategies that can contribute to achieving cultural diversity and building community. Success will depend on the degree to which we implement the agenda.

Agenda Item One: Conduct an institutional audit or assessment to determine the current level of cultural diversity on the campus. Green (1989) offered sample worksheets and checklists to assist in the process. Moreover, Hughes (1987) presented six hierarchical levels of diversity and suggested that campuses attempt to achieve Level 6, building the human community. At Level 6, ethnic differences are embraced, diversity is celebrated, and differences are transcended to construct a genuine community. It is imperative that institutions determine where they are regarding diversity prior to implementing a plethora of scattered programs. The audit or assessment serves as the foundation which colleges and universities can use to begin to achieve cultural diversity.

Agenda Item Two: Define goals for achieving diversity. Goals can be established as a result of the institutional audit or assessment. They serve as the blueprint for achieving diversity. Goals need to be understandable, attainable, measurable, and periodically evaluated. The lack of goals or unclear goals will result in floundered efforts. Progress reports should be made to the governing board, university governance bodies such as faculty senates and university senates, student governments, and centers or task forces representing the needs and interests of African American, Hispanic, Native American, and Asian American students. Failure to report progress on the achievement of cultural diversity can cause many concerned individuals to question the institution's sincerity.

Agenda Item Three: Recruit and retain students from underrepresented racial groups. Recruitment and retention strategies were offered in the previous section of this chapter. These strategies are not unrelated because some of the factors and conditions on the campus which attract students will also help retain them if the conditions are maintained or enhanced. Good academic programs, academic support programs, a critical mass of students from underrepresented racial groups, culturally diverse activities, a hospitable and caring environment, and an identifiable campus location for informal meetings and for socializing and studying are examples of some of the factors and conditions necessary for recruiting and retaining African American, Hispanic, Native American, and Asian American students. The importance of this agenda item cannot be overemphasized.

Agenda Item Four: Identify additional funding sources to provide adequate financial aid to students and to support other diversity efforts. Because state and federal funds for education and financial assistance have decreased during the past decade, alternative sources must be sought and acquired. One of the major reasons cited by students from underrepresented groups for not matriculating in or leaving higher education is inadequate financial resources. The number of scholarships and grants needs to be increased instead of loans which can result in considerable debt.

Agenda Item Five: Recruit and hire faculty and staff members who will actively support a cultural diversity agenda. As we look to the future, it is imperative that we recruit and hire faculty and staff from underrepresented racial groups to serve as role models and mentors for the increased numbers of African American, Hispanic, Native American, and Asian American students who will be recruited. Moreover, the presence of faculty and staff members from these racial groups will attract the students to the institution. Search committees must require evidence of a demonstrated commitment to diversity for all individuals hired by the college or university.

Agenda Item Six: Conduct faculty and staff development activities on cultural diversity. Many current faculty and staff members will need to increase their knowledge about the importance of cultural diversity, racial and cultural differences, the campus climate as perceived by diverse groups, and strategies for ensuring the achievement of the students' academic and personal success. Everyone on the campus has a role to play in achieving cultural diversity. The involvement of the faculty and staff is critical to achieving cultural diversity.

Agenda Item Seven: Establish an academic support program. Because of the inequities in funding and opportunities, many students from underrepresented groups enter higher education without the appropriate levels of preparation. A single academic program or several programs should be established. If one program is established, it is important that steps be taken to prevent the stigmatization of the program and its participants.

Agenda Item Eight: Provide culturally diverse cocurricular and extra-curricular activities. All members of the community can be enriched by these activities. Furthermore, since students who are active tend to be more satisfied with their total educational experiences and are, therefore, more likely to be retained, providing culturally diverse activities and opportunities for involvement are essential. However, students from underrepresented groups should not limit themselves to these activities, they should be invited to participate in a variety of activities and organizations, especially campus programming boards and student governments, where major decisions are made.

Agenda Item Nine: Offer a culturally diverse curriculum and library resources. Some colleges and universities have developed required courses on cultural diversity or multiculturalism. Others have identified courses which already exist and have encouraged all students to select courses from the list. The resources in the library must support the content of the courses. It is imperative that books, journals, and other educational resources be available. Including cultural diversity in the curriculum represents a statement by the institution that underrepresented racial groups are an important part of the campus and society.

Agenda Item Ten: Infuse cultural diversity into the physical environment of the campus. Aside from the obvious inclusion of African American, Hispanic, American Indian, and Asian American students, administrators, and faculty and staff members, the diversity of the campus should be evident in products sold in the bookstore; food service menus (Henley, 1990); and the names of academic buildings, meeting rooms, and residence halls. Prospective students from underrepresented racial groups will find these factors extremely attractive, and these factors will help to engender feelings of pride and affiliation in the students that could help retain them once they enroll.

Agenda Item Eleven: Work with the city or town officials to provide more culturally diverse services and consumer products. Students from underrepresented groups will be members not only of the campus community, but the surrounding community as well. University personnel will need to communicate the importance of diversity to the university and the outside community, and work to ensure the availability of services and products such as the following: newly released culturally diverse movies; culturally diverse music in the music stores and on the local radio stations; hair stylists who are trained to work with a variety of hair textures; cable television networks (e.g., Black Entertainment Network); and health care providers and law enforcement agents who are sensitive to members of underrepresented racial groups.

Agenda Item Twelve: Manage any conflict that could result from efforts to achieve diversity. Unfortunately, everyone will not agree with the direction in which the campus is moving, and there will be many interests competing for the same, limited resources. Therefore, it may be necessary to establish mediation boards to resolve conflicts. If conflicts escalate and result in harassment or hate crimes, it will be imperative that members of the community act expeditiously to address these infractions of the law. The inclusion of all sectors of the campus and surrounding community in the development of plans to achieve diversity could mitigate the negative impact of some disagreements.

Agenda Item Thirteen: Conduct longitudinal, developmental research on underrepresented racial groups. The research should determine needs, identify factors necessary for success, and determine educational outcomes. Hughes (1987) recommended research that would expand knowledge of African American students:

1. Attitudes of [w]hite students toward [African Americans]

2. The willingness of [w]hites to participate in student development programs for diversity

3. Learning styles of [African Americans]

4. Healthy environments that promote diverse communities

5. Developmental research of other ethic minorities (p. 543).

Without such data, we will continue to experiment with methods, some of which may be detrimental to students' academic survival on the campus.

Agenda Item Fourteen: Deliberately prepare all students for diversity on and beyond the campus. Students, regardless of race, need to see African Americans, Hispanics, Native Americans, and Asian Americans at faculty, staff, and administrative levels of the college or university. Student affairs professionals need to educate and prepare students for the work force and a pluralistic society by offering cultural diversity training programs and providing students with certificates of completion that can be included on their resumes. Provide all students with data to help dispel some of the misconceptions they carry (i.e., give them data on higher education enrollment trends for African American students to dispel the affirmative action misconception that African Americans are the only ones getting accepted; challenge students to look around their classrooms and count the number of students from underrepresented racial groups). Encourage joint projects and activities among different racial groups. Make room and floor assignments in the residence halls to promote diversity. Develop a mechanism for the mediation of student-to-student conflicts. We can help shape the future behavior and attitudes of students by engaging them in structured and unstructured activities and creating opportunities for positive interactions.

Agenda Item Fifteen: Reward major efforts to achieve cultural diversity on the campus. It is important to acknowledge and reward successful efforts (Green, 1989). We need to reward that which we value. Award ceremonies, press releases, additional resources, and other forms of recognition could be used to communicate how much we value cultural diversity in the campus community.

CONCLUSION

Colleges and universities will undergo many changes as we move into the 21st century. Changes are evident already in some universities' increased enrollment of students from underrepresented racial groups. As world and national events, including the changing demographics, continue to evolve, colleges and universities will change. "Organizations of higher education are almost totally dependent on the basic lifestyle of their consumers, not only for their service delivery system, but also for their own existence as institutions" (Abede, 1991, p. 29). Some of the changes we can expect to see include a more diverse student population, staff, and faculty; the inclusion of culturally diverse ideas in the curriculum; and more members of underrepresented racial groups participating in university and student decision-making processes which govern policies and procedures.

These changes will not come easily. As is the case with most social change, there will be challenges and conflict will accompany the change. There will be fierce competition for limited resources and conflict over the direction in which the institution is headed. Advocates of the status quo will struggle to maintain tradition and perhaps privileges. Disunity will be evident. However, these may be necessary steps in the evolutionary process of achieving diversity and community.

Including cultural diversity in the university's mission statement will help legitimize cultural diversity on the campus and quell some of the conflict. It will be necessary to hire administrators who are able to manage diversity and implement the revised mission statements (Abede, 1991), hence a bright future for most student development professionals who generally possess highly trained skills in communications and interpersonal relationships.

The future of cultural diversity will be determined by the degree to which we can successfully meet the challenges and implement the agenda for change. Given the measures already underway on many campuses, the future of cultural diversity will be bright. The academy, its members, and the entire nation will be enriched, and our campuses will become models for community building and achieving cultural diversity.

References

A turnabout on civil rights. (1991, November 4). *Newsweek,* p. 32.

Abede, K. (1991, October 10). Managing higher education in the year 2000. *Black Issues in Higher Education,* p. 29.

Abudu, M. (1991, August 29). Current trends in diversity issues affecting higher education. *Black Issues in Higher Education,* pp. 46-49, 52, 54-55.

Allen, W.R. (1988). Black students in U.S. higher education: Toward improved access, adjustment, and achievement. *The Urban Review,* 20(3), 165-188.

American Council on Education. (1991, October 7). Administration rejects civil rights proposal. *Higher Education & National Affairs,* p.6.

Blacks' college picks altered due to racism. (1990, May 28). *Jet,* p. 24.

Carter, D.J., and Wilson, R. (1991). *Ninth annual status report: Minorities in higher education.* Washington, D.C.: American Council on Education.

Cockburn, A. (1991, May 27). Beat the devil: Bush & p.c.— A conspiracy so immense... *The Nation,* pp. 1, 690-691, 704-705.

Conciatore, J. (1991, May 23). Political correctness: A new tyranny or a dangerous diversion? *Black Issues in Higher Education,* pp. 1, 8, 9-11.

Delgado, R. (1991, September 18). Regulation of hate speech may be necessary to guarantee equal protection of all citizens. *The Chronicle of Higher Education*, pp. B1-2.

Farrell, C. (1988, January 27). Black students seen facing "new racism" on many campuses. *The Chronicle of Higher Education*, pp. A1, A36-38.

Farrell, W.C., Jr., and Jones, C.K. (1988). Recent racial incidents in higher education: A preliminary perspective. *The Urban Review*, 20(3), 211-223.

Flaherty, R. (1991, May 16). Adopt anti-harassment rule, Illinois bar advises colleges. *Chicago Sun-Times*, p. 12.

Green, M.F., (Ed.). (1989). *Minorities on campus: A handbook for enhancing diversity.* Washington, D.C.: American Council on Education.

Gunnings, B.B. (1982). Stresses on minority administrators on predominantly white campuses. *Minority Voices*, 5, 29-35.

Heller, S. (1991, September 18). Scholars form group to combat malicious distortions by conservatives. *The Chronicle of Higher Education*, pp. A19-20.

Henley, B. (1990). Unity through diversity week: Promoting diversity and addressing racism. *NASPA Journal*, 27(4), 313-318.

Henley, B. (1991). Anti-harassment and restrictive speech codes: A necessary infringement? *Faculty Bulletin*, Northern Illinois University, 54(5), 7-10.

Hughes, M.S. (1987). Black students' participation in higher education. *Journal of College Student Personnel,* 28(6), 532-545.

Jaschik, S. (1991, December 11). Secretary seeks ban on grants reserved for specific groups. *The Chronicle of Higher Education,* pp. A1, A26-27.

Kuh, G.D., Schuh, J.H., Whitt, E.J., Andreas, R.E., Lyons, J.W., Strange, C.C., Krehbiel, L.E., and MacKay, K.A. (1991). *Involving colleges: Successful approaches to fostering student learning and development outside the classroom.* San Francisco: Jossey-Bass.

Lomotey, K. (1990, April). The retention of African-American students: The effects of institutional arrangements in higher education. Paper presented at the meeting of the American Research Association, Boston, Massachusetts.

Louis, E.T., (1987, August). Racism on campus. *Essence,* pp. 53, 120, 122.

McCauley, D.P., (1988). Effects on specific factors on blacks' persistence at a predominantly white university. *Journal of College Student Development,* 29, 48-51.

The Nation, institutions: Administrators' views of challenges facing institutions in the next five years. (1991, August 28). *The Chronicle of Higher Education Almanac,* p. 38.

O'Brien, E.M. (1988, May 15). Dr. Charles Willie prescribes mentoring methodologies for minorities. *Black Issues in Higher Education,* p. 15.

Saufley, R.W., Cowan, K.O., and Blake, J.H. (1983). The struggles of minority students at predominantly white institutions. In J.H. Connes, III, J.F. Noonan and D. Janha (Eds.), *Teaching minority students* (pp. 3-15). San Francisco: Jossey-Bass.

Wright, D.J., Butler, A., Switzer, V.A., and Masters, J.G. (1988). The future of minority retention. In M.C. Terrell and D.J. Wright (Eds.), *From survival to success: Promoting minority student retention* (pp. 99-131). Washington, D.C.: National Association of Student Personnel Administrators, Inc.

CHAPTER TWO

Cultural Diversity in Residence Halls
Institutional Character and
Promotional Strategies

Melvin C. Terrell
John R. Hoeppel

As colleges struggle with ways to respond to the challenges of diversity on campus, the residence hall is increasingly seen as both a natural and necessary place to intervene. On most university campuses, the residence hall is the place where new students interact daily and most intimately with each other. It is the central context in which diversity becomes real for most students. Different communication styles, different values, and different ethnic identifications all move from the realm of the abstract to that of the concrete in the residence hall. Incoming freshman students often bring a limited exposure to other peoples, lifestyles, and ideas. They are introduced to fellow residents who may be of different color, come from different cultures, or potentially speak different languages. How do institutions respond to this situation?

The research described in this chapter was undertaken to examine how institutions are responding to the challenges that cultural diversity presents in university residence halls. How important are issues of cultural diversity to institutions? How extensively do colleges and universities take advantage of the opportunities to provide multicultural programming for residence hall populations? How much attention is devoted to diversity and multicultural programming in general and to whom is it targeted? Senior student affairs officers at institutions within NASPA Region IV-East were asked these questions about their own institutions. Their responses provide concrete information about the actions behind the rhetoric.

Why are residence halls important to consider in relation to diversity? The literature on residence halls indicates that they are dynamic elements of the overall college experience, capable of exerting strong influences on students' perceptions and behavior (Schroeder & Jackson, 1988; Scheuermann & Grandner, 1986; Waldo, 1986; Wencel, 1985; Conroy, 1982). From this perspective, residence halls represent a prime opportunity to promote issues of cultural diversity in an attempt to play a developmentally positive role in influencing students' perspectives and future behavior.

Given the importance of the residence hall environment, it is enlightening to examine how institutions utilize residence halls to influence the development of a tolerant perspective on campus. Many reported the establishment of multicultural components in their general new student orientations (Collison, 1988) and an increasing number have instituted course requirements that explore issues related to race (Magner, 1990). However, a review of the literature reveals little information about developing multicultural initiatives specifically for residence life programs.

CULTURAL DIVERSITY QUESTIONNAIRE

The primary purpose of this investigation was to collect data on present institutional attitudes and initiatives regarding diversity issues on residential campuses. The authors developed the Cultural Diversity Questionnaire to examine the amount and nature of institutional attention given to multicultural issues and the kinds of programming implemented in the past and planned for the future. The survey examined both campus-wide efforts as well as those targeted at residence halls in particular. Finally, institutional, administrative, and historical characteristics were examined to explore whether these variables influenced the development and provision of multicultural programming on college campuses.

The five-page survey was comprised of 36 questions designed to elicit information in the following four categories:

❏ Institutional Characteristics

❏ Extent of Efforts to Promote Cultural Diversity on Campus

❏ The Administrative Structure of Respondent Institutions

❏ Background Variables of the Individual Respondents

The survey sample was comprised of all of the institutions
within NASPA Region IV-East. (The region includes
Illinois, Indiana, Iowa, Ontario, West Virginia, and
Wisconsin.) The sample was restricted to a single region to
minimize geographical and regional differences. Region
IV-East includes a diverse mix of large and small, urban and
rural, public and private schools, including both highly
diverse and homogeneous student populations.

All senior student affairs officers at institutions in Region
IV-East were sent a copy of the Cultural Diversity
Questionnaire in March of 1990 and were asked to respond
themselves or designate a more appropriate individual within
their institution to respond. After three weeks, a second
survey packet was sent to those institutions not yet responding
to the first mailing.

Institutional Characteristics
Of the 232 institutions surveyed, 77 percent (179) returned
completed surveys. The overall characteristics of the
respondent institutions are presented in Table 1. Almost half
of the respondents were private and approximately one-third
were public 4-year institutions. Almost 80 percent of the
respondents had residential student populations. Of the
institutions responding to the survey, the mean student

Table 1
Characteristics of Respondent Institutions

Institution type (percentages):

                49.7 Private, four-year
                34.6 Public, four-year
                12.3 Community college
                3.4   Other

Student population (percentages):

                79.3 Residential
                18.4 Commuter

Total student population:

                Mean = 8,601
                Range = 90 – 72,000
                sd = 11,146.9

Total residence hall population:

                Mean = 1,956
                Range = 9 – 12,000
                sd = 2,208.76

Ethnic distribution of students
(mean percentages):

                2.5   Asian
                6.01 African American
                85.88 Caucasian
                3.92 Hispanic
                1.81 Native American
                3.69 International
                6.21 Other

population was 8,601 and the mean residence hall population was 1,956.

Ethnic Diversity in Residence Halls

The reported distribution of ethnic backgrounds is also presented in Table 1. The responding institutions serve a fairly diverse collection of students. They are also active campuses; 77 percent reported active student clubs or organizations associated with at least half of the ethnic groups represented on campus.

Respondents detailed the ethnic diversity of their staffs as well as that of their student populations. Results indicated that student populations were more diverse than staff populations at the responding institutions. Only 21 percent of the respondents reported that the ethnic composition of their overall staff matched that of the student population; 36 percent reported a staff that "partially matched" the student diversity (being somewhat diverse, but not as fully as the student body), while 40 percent indicated that the diversity within the staff did not match that of the student body.

Over two-thirds (69 percent) of respondents reported that the ethnic composition of students within their residence halls was similar to that of their overall student population. Also 31 percent reported a residence advisor (RA) staff matched in backgrounds to the student body, 34 percent a "partially matched" RA staff, and 35 percent a situation where the RA staff did not match the student profile.

Campus Efforts to Promote Cultural Diversity

Having described the overall characteristics of the responding institutions and the ethnic diversity of their students and staffs, the Cultural Diversity Questionnaire also examined current attitudinal and programmatic initiatives toward the promotion of cultural awareness.

Campus Attitudes

It is clear from the survey results that addressing cultural diversity is a major issue in the minds of senior student affairs officers. Over 78 percent of the respondents rated cultural diversity as important or very important (top two ratings on a 5-point Likert scale) on their campuses. Fifty-four percent of the respondents indicated that cultural diversity issues received much attention (top two ratings on 5-point scale) in the general campus environment. As for diversity issues specifically in student residence halls, the amount of emphasis declined: 43 percent reported much attention (top two ratings on 5-point scale), 35 percent chose the middle rating, and 22 percent reported minimal attention (bottom two ratings).

General campus perceptions of the importance of cultural diversity are not affected by whether the institution is publicly or privately funded, but the attention devoted to such issues specifically in residence halls is related to this characteristic. Publicly funded institutions reported significantly more attention given to cultural diversity issues in residence halls than did privately funded institutions (F=3.98, p=.004).

Additionally, residential institutions gave more attention across the general campus environment to issues of cultural diversity than did commuter institutions (F=7.21, p=.008).

Past Programming Efforts

To what extent do institutions act on their reported belief that diversity is an important issue? Results indicated an overwhelming proportion of campuses has been responding to this perceived need. Ninety-two percent of the respondents reported that their institutions had sponsored programs aimed at enhancing awareness of cultural diversity in the overall campus environment during the past two years. Sixty percent reported sponsoring such programs specifically in student residence halls.

What kinds of efforts are currently being made to promote understanding of diversity? Sponsoring special events to celebrate different cultures was the most common means of attempting to raise awareness of diversity, with 89 percent of institutions involved in such efforts. Seventy-two percent of respondents reported providing workshops and training sessions to various constituencies about diversity issues, while 31 percent reported developing courses in the academic curriculum and 22 percent reported other efforts. (It may be noted that sponsoring special cultural events is relatively easy for most institutions with active student clubs and organizations. Developing a delivery system for multicultural workshops or revising course syllabi or program requirements involve considerably more energy and institutional commitment.)

To whom are these programs targeted? Diversity efforts were most commonly aimed at students in general (not restricted specifically to student residents or any other subpopulation), with 84 percent of institutions reporting such approaches. Additionally, 67 percent reported programming aimed specifically for administrators, 64 percent targeted faculty, and 54 percent reported programming designed for residence hall assistants and staff.

Residence hall students were the primary audience at only 32 percent of responding institutions, with an additional 25 percent working with other audiences (including students' parents and community members). It must be noted that these reports of targeted audiences were not mutually exclusive;

many institutions reported different efforts aimed at multiple audiences. When asked to describe the events they perceive as most successful, the most common response was social and cultural special events. There was no clear pattern of responses beyond this particular finding for effectiveness.

Another measure of an institution's commitment to promoting a multicultural environment is the degree to which colleges enable and encourage diversity within the circles of student leadership. On this score, respondents said that minority students were encouraged to become student leaders in more than two-thirds (69 percent) of their campuses, and almost all reported components of their RA staff training programs devoted to enhancing cultural diversity (23 percent giving it major emphasis, 57 percent reporting some time spent on diversity, and 19 percent indicating it was at least a minor topic).

Future Plans
Respondents were asked to describe their campuses' future plans to develop programs to promote cultural understanding during the next two years. Fully 87 percent of respondents reported that their institutions were indeed planning efforts to enhance the understanding of diversity. (Interestingly though, this figure is 5 percentage points lower than those who have already sponsored such efforts in the past two years.) Programs designed for students were again the most common approach underlying future plans, with 81 percent planning programs for students, 64 percent planning programs for faculty and staff, and 63 percent planning efforts for residence hall advisors.

When queried about the nature of their future programming efforts, 78 percent of institutions reported

planning special events to celebrate different cultures,
followed by significantly fewer institutions developing
elective courses (41 percent) and even fewer developing
required courses in the academic curriculum (16 percent).
This pattern of focusing on special events, followed to a lesser
extent by workshops and course development, reflects the
history of past programming efforts at such campuses.
Previous comments on the relative ease of celebration versus
workshop development or course revision may be appropriate
here. In short, most campuses are planning variations on
previously undertaken approaches.

Effects of Size of the Overall Student Body
Because the size of an institution was hypothesized to be a
key measure of a school's ability to respond to varying needs,
the size of the total student body was examined as an
independent variable in relation to the perceived importance
of diversity issues, the attention such issues receive both in
the general campus environment and specifically within
residence halls, past histories of programming efforts, and
commitments for future programming plans. Institutions
were grouped into thirds based on the size of their total student
bodies: small (less than 2,000 students), medium
(2,000-7,775 students), and large (7,775+ students) schools.
As expected, there were significant differences in attitudes
and experiences between the size groupings of these
institutions; complete results are presented in Table 2.
Overall, larger institutions perceived diversity issues as more
important, gave them more attention in the general campus
environment, more attention in residence halls, and were
more likely to report past programming efforts both across
the general campus environment and specifically in residence
hall settings.

Table 2
Effects of Total School Population on the Promotion of Cultural Diversity Programming Across the Campus Environment

Dependent Variable	F	df	Signif
V1. Importance of issue on campus	4.27	2	.009**
V2. Attention on campus in general	5.89	2	.003 ***
V3. Attention in residence halls	17.33	2	.000 ***
V4. Past programs in general	5.21	2	.006 **
V5. Past programs for residence hall	5.68	2	.004 **
V16. Plans to develop future programs	6.39	2	.002 **
V17. Future programs for students	4.63	2	.011 *
V18. Future programs for RAs	1.44	2	.241
V19. Future programs for faculty/staff	3.53	2	.031
V20. Future programs for elective courses	3.91	2	.022
V21. Future programs for required courses	1.26	2	.285

* $p < .05$
** $p < .01$
*** $p < .001$

The overall trend is clearly that larger institutions have been more directly involved in promoting diversity as an issue in the college experience. Interestingly however, when it came to detailing specific future plans for impacting particular target populations, results became much less pronounced, often nonsignificant (variables V17 through

V21 in Table 2). Although the involvement of larger institutions in past efforts is clear, results are much less indicative of differences in specific future initiatives.

Effects of Size of Residence Hall Population

Next, the research examined size as it relates specifically to the numbers of students in residence halls; large institutions may only have small residential populations, and small schools may be highly residential; overall size measures would tend to cover these differences. It was expected that the size of an institution's residential population would likely drive the extent and variety of its residence life programs. Respondents were asked to report the number of students living in residence halls and, as above, institutions were divided into thirds based on the size of the student population living in residence halls. These size groupings were examined in relation to the same collection of dependent variables detailed above; complete results are presented in Table 3.

Overall, there were major effects of the size of the residence hall population on the perceived importance of diversity issues, the attention given such issues within residence halls, and the likelihood of programming efforts in residence halls during the past two years. In each of these cases, the effect was positive: institutions with larger resident populations perceived diversity as more important, gave it more attention, and offered more programming initiatives to promote its awareness.

Additionally, there was a major effect of the size of the residence hall population on future plans to provide cultural diversity training to residence hall advisors (schools with

Table 3
Effects of Size of Residence Hall Population on the
Promotion of Cultural Diversity Programming

Dependent Variable	F	df	Signif
V1. Importance of issue on campus	5.33	2	.006**
V2. Attention on campus in general	3.77	2	.026*
V3. Attention in residence halls	13.55	2	.000***
V4. Past Programs in general	2.52	2	.084
V5. Past Programs for residence hall	6.94	2	.001***
V16. Plans to develop future programs	3.47	2	.034*
V17. Future programs for students	3.11	2	.048*
V18. Future programs for RAs	7.60	2	.001***
V19. Future programs for faculty/staff	1.77	2	.174
V20. Future programs for elective courses	3.20	2	.044
V21. Future programs for required courses	3.30	2	.040

* p < .05
** p < .01
*** p < .001

larger resident populations being more likely to initiate RA diversity training), but only a moderate effect on future plans to provide programs for students. It may be that most of these institutions already have provided programs for students, and that additional or expanded efforts were now targeted primarily for advisors. There was also a moderate effect of residence hall population size on future planning for developing elective and required courses on cultural diversity (again, schools with larger resident populations having been more likely to be considering the development of courses as a vehicle to promote an understanding of diversity).

Effects of Heterogeneity on Programming Efforts
Is the amount of minority representation in the student population related to the extent or nature of multicultural programming initiatives? It was hypothesized that those campuses with highly mixed student bodies would be more sensitive to and more active in promoting diversity. To study this, racial/ethnic heterogeneity within the student body was examined with respect to its effects on past initiatives and future plans to promote cultural diversity.   Respondents reported the ethnic breakdown of their student populations in percentages. To better utilize these numbers, the data were recoded to low (less than 10 percent), moderate (11-24 percent) and high (25+ percent) proportions for each distinct ethnic group.

Overall, simply dividing institutions by the variation in the sizes of various ethnic groups did not provide many insights into differences in multicultural programming. Specifically, variations in the percentages of different ethnic groups on campus showed little effect on any of the attitudinal or programming variables examined.

Because of the expected preponderance of white students on most campuses, however, looking at the overall proportion of Caucasian students provided a more useful perspective. Institutions with lower proportions of white students obviously had higher proportions of minority students; therefore the proportion of white students was used as a global measure of overall heterogeneity within any given institution. This approach provided one of the few significant findings related to the relative size of minority representation within the student body: the amount of general attention given to issues of cultural diversity was related to lower proportions of Caucasian students ($F=3.18$, $df=2$, $p=.044$). In other words, the amount of attention devoted to issues of cultural diversity in the general campus environment was higher in institutions with higher minority populations. These institutions tend to spend more time trying to promote cultural diversity among both students and staff. It should be noted that although this finding confirms what might seem obvious, the size of this effect is only moderate.

Contrary to expectation, the size of the minority population on campus did not seem to affect the amount of attention given to diversity issues specifically in residence halls, the extent of past programming initiatives, nor a commitment to develop future plans for promotion of cultural issues. The reasons for this are unclear.

In the only other finding related to heterogeneity in the student body, the proportion of international students was highly related to a history of past programming efforts within residence halls. Those institutions with higher numbers of international students were more likely to report such efforts in their residence facilities ($F=5.79$, $df=2$, $p=.004$). This effect may be a response to the obvious need for students new to the United States to become acclimated to their new surroundings, and to the related needs of local students to understand the varied cultural backgrounds present in residence halls with high proportions of foreign exchange students. Eisen (1986) described the importance of such needs and detailed how institutions could facilitate positive interactions for these students. As she reported, such efforts were most effective when woven into the fabric of residence life programs.

Administrative Structures
The present research also explored the administrative structures responsible for overseeing multicultural programming within residence halls.

Of the responding institutions, an overwhelming proportion of schools (94 percent) vested responsibility for student housing within student affairs divisions, with only 4.6 percent relying upon academic affairs, and 1.3 percent with "other" administrative arrangements.

Half of the respondents had a separate budget line item for staff development within the student affairs division. Almost as many (43 percent) entrusted staff development in areas of ethnic and cultural differences to a committee structure. However, only approximately one-sixth (17 percent) of the sample had an office directly responsible for addressing cultural and ethnic issues in student housing. In a possibly related finding, almost half of the responding institutions had an Office of Minority Affairs on campus. It may be that any programming to promote diversity in residence halls on these campuses was monitored by the Office of Minority Affairs.

Outreach efforts to the surrounding community regarding cultural issues were common, with 58 percent of the sample reporting such activities.

Backgrounds of Individuals Responding to the Survey
As mentioned earlier, this survey was specifically addressed to senior student affairs officers at NAPSA Region IV-East institutions. It may be safely assumed that some of the questionnaires were completed by other administrative staff, and, therefore, our demographic and background data reflect a somewhat ill-defined group, best seen as "chief student affairs officers or their designees." Not unexpectedly, the majority of respondents were male (70 percent) and Caucasian (88 percent). The respondents were employed at their present institutions for an average of 10.8 years, having spent an average of 18.0 years in higher education. Finally, results indicated that our respondents practiced what they preached, as 88 percent of the administrators responding to this survey reported participating themselves in programs focusing on issues of cultural or ethnic diversity within the past two years.

Data on the demographic characteristics of those administrators who completed the questionnaire were examined to determine whether they carried any influence in their reports of campus perceptions or policies. Neither the sex nor ethnic group of the respondents was significantly related to perceptions of importance of diversity issues or reports of the attention devoted to such issues on campus.

DISCUSSION

It is clear from the results of the present study that the vast majority of senior student affairs officers perceive cultural diversity as a central issue on their campuses. This concern is evident across the range of institutional characteristics and administrative structures. This may not be surprising with the high degree of attention currently focused on diversity in the public and professional press.

Which institutions are most active in promoting diversity in residence halls? The present results indicate that larger schools and those with larger resident populations are most active. Similarly, those schools with higher minority populations are more likely to actively promote racial and cultural understanding. The most obvious interpretation of these results is that such institutions are more diverse in nature and have more resources to devote to issues that affect them most intimately.

Additionally, the present study indicates that the amount of attention given to diversity issues is higher in public institutions than in private institutions. Institutions with residence hall populations are more likely to devote time and attention to addressing diversity issues than are commuter institutions. This higher degree of attention on residential campuses suggests that such colleges understand that residence halls can act as crucibles for forging multicultural understanding or, alternately, as sources of stress and conflict if such issues are not forthrightly addressed.

The results of the present study also indicate that most institutions are actively involved in some aspect of the development of a multicultural campus environment. However, many institutions are implementing the easier and less costly initiatives: social events, celebrations, special heritage weeks. Less common are multicultural awareness workshops as a required part of the matriculation process or revised academic courses as part of the curriculum.

The lower level of support for workshop and course development may represent institutional economics or politics. Workshop development can be costly in terms of staff training or consultant time. Perhaps more important, delivery vehicles need to be designed to ensure that such workshops reach those individuals most in need. Such programs can be far-reaching and may promote deeper institutional change than does an ethnic heritage celebration. In addition, developing courses in the academic curriculum often requires a thorough review of present course offerings and a faculty-based curricular revision process. Such curricular revision has the potential to spark rigorous debate regarding academic freedom, free speech, and the place of diversity in the curriculum. Many institutions may not be ready to tackle such public discussions; many may not be convinced that curricular revision is an effective way to enhance diversity on their campuses. Until consensus is reached on many of these matters, change in the required curriculum is likely to fall far behind other, more immediate initiatives.

The current study also indicates that most diversity programming is targeted at the general student population rather than at residence hall students. Although all students need exposure to cultural and ethnic issues, institutions may be missing an important and inherently powerful opportunity by not focusing special efforts in the residence halls. The works of Conroy (1982), Schroeder and Jackson (1988), Waldo (1985, 1986), and Wencel (1985) all suggested that the residence hall has provided a unique and powerful opportunity to encourage the development of an open and tolerant understanding of diversity issues.

What kinds of initiatives are effective? Can isolated interventions (e.g., a workshop on cultural differences in communication) lead to significant change in students'

perceptions or behavior? The answers to these questions are
beyond the scope of this project, but others have begun to
explore this issue. Waldo (1985) examined the effectiveness
of interpersonal communications workshops at the University
of Maryland. Results indicated that significant positive
effects on several indices of interpersonal communication
were related to participation in such programs. Additionally,
Terrell (1988) examined the efforts of colleges and
universities to work toward promoting and appreciating other
cultures through programs that highlight diversity. He
pointed to the multicultural mix represented in university
residence halls as an ideal laboratory to test these ideas. From
this perspective, one can reasonably urge proactive initiatives
on multicultural issues within residence halls as potentially
effective intervention strategies.

CONCLUSION

Most institutions view cultural diversity as central to their
missions and devote significant amounts of attention to it. But
the incidence of ethnic or racial conflict is widespread. More
effective means of addressing these issues need to be
developed and residence halls present a unique and powerful
setting in which to address and promote multicultural
perspectives.

References

Collison, M. (1988). For many freshmen, orientation now includes efforts to promote racial understanding. *The Chronicle of Higher Education*, p. A29.

Conroy, W. (1982). Quality of residence hall life. *Journal of College and University Student Housing*, 12(2), 17-20.

Eisen, G.S. (1986). Fostering international understanding: Cross-cultural issues in international residential settings. *NASPA Journal*, 23(4), 55-59.

Magner, D. (1990, June 6). Difficult questions face colleges that require students to take courses that explore issues related to race. *The Chronicle of Higher Education*, p. A29.

Scheuermann, T., and Grandner, D. (1986). Residence hall unit agreements: A step beyond rules and regulations. *Journal of College and University Student Housing*, 16(1), 12-17.

Schroeder, C., and Jackson, G. (1988). Creating conditions for student development in campus living environments. *NASPA Journal*, 25(1), 45-53.

Terrell, M.C. (1988). Racism: Undermining higher education. *NASPA Journal*, 26(2), 82-84.

Waldo, M. (1985). Improving interpersonal communication in a university residential community. *Journal of Humanistic Education and Development*, 23(3), 126-33.

Waldo, M. (1986). Academic achievement and retention as related to student's personal and social adjustment in university residence halls. *Journal of College and University Student Housing*, 16(1), 19-23.

Wencel, J. (1985). A study of the perceived social climate of the residence halls at the University of South Carolina-Columbia. *Carolina Review*, 1(1), 7-10.

CHAPTER THREE

Law Enforcement and Education
New Partners in Diversity

Doris J. Wright

Achieving cultural diversity requires that students, faculty, and staff feel safe and secure enough to explore and to appreciate differences on a daily basis. Bias, bigotry, and prejudice flourish in a climate of fear, intimidation, and threat. These risk factors, in turn, make students powerless and, thus, vulnerable to crime. In addition, learning is impeded, stifled, or severely restricted. Colleges and universities can never hope to educate students adequately when the Ivory Tower is not safe for either teacher or learner. Moreover, how can students be expected to learn to appreciate "difference" when their own difference is neither valued nor respected, leaving them psychologically and/or physically threatened?

Protecting our campuses from physical threat and preventing crime traditionally have been the roles of campus law enforcement personnel. Yet, how traditional law enforcement roles fit into a "new campus world order," one which appreciates diversity and celebrates difference, is not clear. As integral participants of the campus community, campus law enforcement officers have an essential role to play in helping everyone to appreciate their own diversity and to respect diversity in others.

This chapter discusses the roles which campus law enforcement personnel play in campus efforts to achieve the goal of a culturally diverse campus. Achieving this goal requires that campus police officers and other campus law enforcement personnel increase their interactions with student affairs staff, forming a new working alliance not found on most campuses today. This new educational partnership is necessary if colleges are ever to discover the optimum "climate conditions" in which diversity and the appreciation of difference flourish best. Before we can discuss cultural diversity within the context of law enforcement, we must first understand its relationship to safety and crime prevention. A beginning point, however, is to define what is meant by diversity.

DIVERSITY CLIMATE DEFINED

Diversity has many definitions and meanings. Diversity is a set of beliefs concerning the positive value attached to racial, cultural, gender, and other lifestyle differences. Its use within this chapter and its practice on college campuses is comprised of the following key elements which affect developmental growth:

❒ Diversity is learned and reinforced within an environment which assures that a student can feel safe, free of the risk of psychological harm or physical threat.

❒ Such a feeling of safety and security is a necessary condition of empowerment and self-confidence, essential learning tools for any achieving student.

❒ Students who feel empowered and confident are likely to: (a) challenge bias and prejudice with direct and assertive actions; and (b) show willingness to try new ideas, thoughts, or actions which represent the appreciation of different lifestyles, gender, cultural, and racial backgrounds.

❒ Developmental growth gains are best solidified, sustained, and synthesized within a student's lifestyle in a safe, secure and comforting campus environment.

In summary, appreciating diversity and practicing this appreciation is a developmental task for which students can be taught to learn or achieve. As a developmental task of young college students, it is a value which is essential for campuses to teach to developing scholars.

POLICE RESPONSIBILITY FOR DIVERSITY

What responsibility for ensuring diversity can or should law enforcement personnel have on our college and university campuses? First, it may be argued that officers' traditional role of enforcing compliance with local, state, and federal laws helps to define the parameters in which "difference" exists on campus. Minorities, women, and physically challenged students make those affirmations within the parameters of state and federal laws which officers enforce on campus.

Second, each time officers perform their designated service functions, for example, controlling traffic or securing buildings, they help ensure that the campus environment and its students remain open and accessible so that learning about "difference" can take place safely. Third, each time officers arrest an alleged student offender — a drunken driver, a campus burglar, a youthful sex offender — they restore lost safety; by doing so, they help manage the real or perceived psychological and physical threats which can impede learning. Finally, each time officers lecture a student about crime prevention, they seed self-responsibility while teaching risk-appraisal life skills which can strengthen a student's sense of connection and belonging to his or her campus community.

TRADITIONAL ROLES OF CAMPUS LAW ENFORCEMENT

Campus law enforcement administrative units usually include commissioned officers, guards, and civilian employees who perform a variety of service, enforcement, and investigative functions for a college or university. Campus police departments are headed by an administrator, a chief of police and commissioned officer, who reports either directly to the university president or to a vice president.

Commissioned officers are accredited by their respective state law enforcement agencies. Most states require commissioned officers to attend a formal training academy, involving several hundred hours of training and covering such topics as police procedures and order maintenance functions, and requiring their familiarity with state criminal laws and appropriate federal statutes. Several states now require or recommend that their commissioned campus officers have some college education (Peak, 1989). It is not uncommon for many officers on college campuses to possess bachelors' degrees. A select few even have graduate or law degrees. In addition, continuing education is often necessary for some officers to maintain their peace officer certification (Bess & Horton, 1988).

Campus guards and civilian employees share security and traffic control duties with police officers. Guards, for example, may patrol classroom buildings, checking to see if doors are locked or rooms secured; they may issue tickets for illegal parking also. Issuing parking stickers and managing keys may be roles performed by civilian employees or by guards, depending on the size of the campus department and any role restrictions imposed by state law enforcement agencies. Most guards and civilian employees do not go through the extensive law enforcement training nor are they accredited as are commissioned officers (F. Hacker, personal communication, April 1992). Larger college campuses may have separate offices or units for parking and traffic roles, security (making keys and locks), and other safety functions. These units may be distinct from the law enforcement departments.

Regardless of the police department's size or structure, there are roles and functions which most campus officers perform. These are: (1) law enforcement, including arrest powers and criminal investigation; (2) maintenance of campus order; (3) traffic management and control; (4) crime prevention; and (5) providing emergency services, a role which was introduced in the 1970s (Esposito & Stormer, 1989).

While campus police officers engage in routine functions similar to those of their municipal counterparts, often they will interpret and carry out some of these duties differently from their fellow city officers (Nichols, 1985). Campus societal norms; academic, institutional, and environmental characteristics; physical security responsibilities; and administrative constraints combine with other campus climate factors to restrict typical law enforcement functions. Take, for example, the underage college student who is stopped for campus public intoxication. Municipal officers might decide to jail and fine the youthful offender immediately, without providing education about drinking responsibility.

On college campuses where educational interventions are possible, the youthful offender might be referred to the Dean of Students Office for alleged code of conduct violation or required to seek counseling to understand the reasons underlying illegal alcohol consumption. Additionally, he or she might then be required to visit with the alcohol education counselor to discuss the risk factors associated with drinking. All these educational interventions could occur as part of the student's disciplinary actions, and may replace or augment the traditional law enforcement response of arrest and incarceration. Learning about drinking risks and identifying his or her responsibility for such behavior are important developmental life tasks for young students to learn and master.

RELATIONSHIP BETWEEN CAMPUS POLICE AND STUDENT AFFAIRS

While the collaboration between campus law enforcement and student affairs professionals is a natural one, the relationship has not been well defined in the past.

How can student affairs and law enforcement professionals work together on those educational activities which contribute to achieving cultural diversity? Three areas of possible alliance are described briefly below.

Managing Student Discipline

Esposito and Stormer (1989) observed that police officers' investigative skills can enhance the adjudication of student discipline matters, typically a student affairs task. Those offices responsible for managing student discipline, such as the dean of students or residence hall governance, sometimes need law enforcement's investigative capacities to resolve student discipline matters. To the extent that student judicial systems reinforce the mastery of responsibility to self and others, campus officers can and do offer input into discipline sanctions which help students make informed and less risky life decisions, choices which reduce the likelihood that a student will become a repeat offender. In some instances, it might be necessary to impose discipline sanctions rather than jailing them, since developmental growth and learning are far less likely to occur while one is jailed!

Crime Prevention Educators

Each day, campus law enforcement personnel are involved with crime prevention activities. Student affairs staffers, likewise, are concerned with crime prevention and other activities which reduce students' psychological and physical risks, thereby removing a barrier to their learning. Esposito and Stormer (1989) noted, ". . . crime prevention is more than simply nonvictimization. Rather, it involves creating a climate environment where opinions and rights are respected, discussed, analyzed, modified and accepted" (p. 29). Embodied within this definition is the message that respect for "difference," that is to say diversity, is integral to the campus growth and thus is an important educational role in which campus police officers and student affairs professionals alike should involve themselves.

Developmental Educators and Teachers

Enhancing campus climate is an educational mission requiring both student affairs staff and campus law enforcement officers to educate and teach students interventions which will intentionally promote their diversity awareness. Most student development scholars have yet to acknowledge that achieving diversity is a developmental task. Despite this fact, campus police officers and student affairs staff together can teach students how to facilitate mastery of this task.

LAW ENFORCERS OR PUBLIC SERVANTS?

The alliance between campus police officers and student affairs professionals has not been without its problems.

Campus law enforcement personnel and college administrators have failed to agree on the proper balance between
the officers' dual roles of law enforcement and public service
(Nichols, 1985). Some administrators prefer a strong law
enforcement presence, including arrest authority, while others
want officers to engage in service activities primarily,
de-emphasizing the arrest responsibilities.

In municipal police forces, most of a city officer's time
(80 percent) is spent in service functions; campus police
expend a similar proportion of their time engaged in campus
service (Nichols, 1987). Powell (cited in Nichols, 1987)
noted that "defining the proper role and function of a campus
security [police] department is difficult because the operation
must be programmed to meet the needs and general attitudes
of the campus it will serve. However, any campus department
must direct its efforts primarily at prevention and service to
be successful" (p. 21). Such comments support the need to
balance these essential service roles and law enforcement
functions and suggest that officers' actions should promote
the educational and learning ideals of their own institution.
Moreover, police officers should emphasize learning and
instruction while ensuring a safe and secure campus
environment, both physically and socially. This
accomplishment will promote social and educational
exchange among students (Esposito & Stormer, 1989). By
fulfilling this service role, officers thereby promote diversity.
Student affairs professionals and campus police officers
together with administrators must nurture a social
environment which celebrates the diversity of cultures
through a multitude of extra-curricular activities (Esposito &
Stormer, 1989).

In summary, student affairs professionals do interact with campus law enforcement personnel frequently. As educators and professionals, both are concerned with creating a safe campus environment, one conducive to student learning and growth and the mastery of diversity tasks. It is within such context that the alliance between police and student affairs professionals is born and will grow. Since both groups are committed to enhancing the campus climate for students, staff, and faculty, what then is the role of police in enhancing a climate that embraces cultural diversity?

NEW LAW ENFORCEMENT
DIVERSITY ROLES

Dozens of scholars have written about cultural climate and diversity. None, until now, have recommended roles for campus law enforcement personnel that will promote or encourage the development of diversity. The responsibility of law enforcement officers for diversity extends beyond simply being present to maintain order at a free speech rally or taking photographs of those students who voice opposition to governmental policies. One must ask: Is the police role ended once it has assured classroom doors are locked and traffic is flowing smoothly? These and other campus situations reflect routine police duties that can either support or restrict diversity depending upon circumstances, as suggested in earlier discussions.

Beyond the mandated law enforcement roles and typical service duties, what place do campus police have in ensuring a favorable and open cultural climate, a campus where acceptance of difference is assured? A few suggestions for new or expanded roles for campus law enforcement are offered below.

Recruiters of Minority Students

As state and federal statutes make demands, and as the public outcry for equal access to higher learning opportunities for minorities, women, and the physically challenged grows louder each year, colleges and universities struggle to recruit, retain, and graduate these special students. Increasingly, institutions are searching for "slick," packaged recruiting devices with which to attract minorities and other special groups to campuses. Rarely are campus police officers asked to participate in minority recruiting activities, but perhaps there is a role for their participation.

Consider an example from this real-life scenario at a large southwestern university: During a recruiting activity for minority student scholars and their families, several concerned parents asked questions about the institution's safety and security procedures. Another parent asked about sexual assault prevention programs and other safety activities for her incoming freshman daughter. An alert counselor suggested that these parents pose their questions to the campus officer who was on duty outside the auditorium. To the surprise of the officer and the delight of the counselor, these assertive parents did indeed ask the officer several safety questions (D. Wright, personal communication, April 1992).

The larger issue remains: Why were no campus officers invited to participate in these orientation activities? Why shouldn't minority parents be as concerned as other parents about their children's safety in college? Clearly, planners omitted a significant recruiting tool, the importance of safety, when attempting to attract these talented students to campus.

For minorities whose home communities do not have favorable impressions of law enforcement, seeing an officer supporting rather than harassing their son or daughter is an important social modeling for parents, students, and officers alike.

As campuses wrestle with increased reports of and actual incidences of sexual assault and racially motivated hate crimes, the concerns of crime prevention and public safety are on the minds of many incoming minority students and their parents. Perhaps institutions should incorporate safety and crime prevention as special recruiting tools for minority students and include officers in the recruiting process. If learning about crime prevention and personal safety is an essential developmental task that facilitates self-responsibility, belonging and comfort, then it would seem natural for campus police officers to be involved in all recruiting and retention activities for minorities.

Contributors to Policy Development

Colleges still have difficulty writing policies which effectively describe appropriate adult behaviors for students, without restricting their right to freedom of expression. No wonder that campuses have poorly conceived policies describing behaviors which constitute racial and/or sexual harassment and protecting students from undue risk of sexual assault.

College administrators do not hesitate to seek the input of lawyers as they write these policy statements, but they do not seek input from those whose duty it is to enforce those policies daily — campus officers. It seems logical that officers, in combination with teaching faculty and along with student affairs professionals, should tackle these policies collaboratively. Officers' input and investigative insights could facilitate new definitions of conduct and behavior, especially concerning codes of conduct relating to alleged crimes such as sexual assault or robbery.

Moreover, most student discipline policies are woefully inadequate in the policies governing the use (or misuse) of computer technology and behavioral misconduct on the terminal. Campus racial or gender harassment policies, for example, often do not extend to the use of computers as tools for harassment.

Campus law enforcement personnel can become a powerful new voice as colleges struggle to redefine their policies in ways which affirm diversity and encourage respect for difference while at the same time reassuring the campus community about its safety. Campus police officers and other security personnel have new roles awaiting them as they provide guidance to deans of students, vice presidents and college deans, and as these officials work to amend, revise, and/or develop campus policies which protect students, staff, and faculty from racial and gender harassment. Campus law enforcement professionals should be included in all discussions regarding such discipline matters and participate in the "brainstorming sessions" regarding policy development. Again, the law enforcement collaboration with student affairs professionals can be a successful partnership, with the staffs of judicial affairs, residence halls, student activities, and deans of students joining upper administration and campus police to create clearly defined student discipline policies and educational sanctions and interventions. The outcome for such interdepartmental collaboration is one which affirms diversity across the campus equitably.

Crime Prevention Educators

This role is certainly not a new one for officers; they conduct dozens of crime prevention and public safety lectures each year on topics ranging from locking doors to campus lighting to sexual assault prevention to environmental safety. Less frequently have officers been asked to advise student groups about how to have a safe protest march, how to manage protest opposition actions, or how to protect a pro-choice sandwich board from destruction. Student organizations rarely discuss such crime prevention and self-protection measures until after an incident has occurred.

Officers can help teach students how to recognize and report racially motivated criminal activity. Officers could become consultants or advisors to student groups as they plan social events to learn effective ways to manage a drunk/disruptive attendee while protecting the organization's liability.

Since crime prevention is a life skill which our campuses do not teach regularly, officers can play a significant role in helping students learn self-responsibility and self-protection. An ideal collaboration is for officers to team together with staffs from residence halls, fraternities/sororities, judicial entities, campus activities and others to create leadership workshops which train leaders of such organizations to assume responsibility for their membership's safety. In doing so, those groups who have never trusted police or those who have never appreciated an officer's educational roles may learn new ways for their membership to interact with campus law enforcement, before a crisis arises. These learning activities alter students' impressions about uncaring and insensitive officers, thus challenging a stereotype. For the police officers, their preconceptions about certain student groups, that is, minorities, gays, fraternities, may be changed, too, thereby removing a bias from the officers' minds Thus, involving law enforcement in students' learning is beneficial in one distinct way: mutual understanding, a condition which most assuredly will enhance the overall campus cultural climate.

BENEFITS AND CHALLENGES OF INVOLVEMENT IN ACHIEVING DIVERSITY

In the future campus law enforcement personnel will be asked to assume new service roles which encourage students' mastery of diversity skills. These new, as yet undefined educational roles await campus officers if they are freed to involve themselves in these service tasks. The common thread among these new roles is one which promotes collaboration with other campus offices to fulfill the goal of a culturally open and diverse campus community. This diversity thread will become the unifying force which guides officers and student affairs professionals alike to seek work collaborations. Of course, these new or expanded roles come with benefits and risks for the officer, the law enforcement profession, and for the institution, all of which must be understood before officers can participate effectively in diversity interventions. These new roles along with their potential benefits and challenges are briefly described below.

Diversity Training
The student population of our future college campuses will be more racially or ethnically diverse than ever (American Council on Education, 1988). This "browning" of our campuses requires that educators, including law enforcement

personnel, interact with a wide range of racial, cultural, and ethnic groups. Officers and law enforcement departments who choose to participate in campus diversity must first make sure they themselves are free of bias. This feat is not an easy one, to be sure. While some students would debate this statement, campus law enforcement personnel are role models for young adults. Their responsibility for ensuring diversity demands that their departments first must look internally at their own racism, gender bias, ageism, homophobia, and other biases and remedy those ills, lest they model bias and bigotry to students.

Campus law enforcement departments should create or develop diversity training activities for their commissioned officers and security guards, as well as their civilian staff. All staff from guard to officer to police chief should be required to complete such training. Diversity awareness skills should be an essential criteria for advancement or promotion.

Achieving these staff development objectives is difficult when campus financial resources for police departments are dwindling. Nonetheless, campus law enforcement departments are encouraged to exercise assertiveness and creativity as they develop diversity training. The easiest way to ensure that officers have these diversity skills is to integrate their development into police training academies, require cadets to learn diversity skill training and conflict management as an essential work skill necessary to become a commissioned peace officer. At present few police training academies, accreditation agencies, or state licensing boards are required by state law to provide diversity training for their officers. Yet, as our state legislatures, our colleges, and our home communities reflect increased racial and cultural diversity, such training is likely to become a requirement in the future.

New Professional Roles
Within a college environment where degrees, professional skills, and credentials are important, campus law enforcement officers can increase their professionalism by enhancing their interpersonal skills in intercultural communication or diversity awareness. If diversity awareness were included in the criteria for leadership promotion, it would set an important trend on campuses that might motivate teaching faculty and professional staff to follow suit, thereby strengthening the academic integrity of faculty, staff, and officers alike. As campus law enforcement departments adopt diversity roles and realign their administrative staff to accommodate these new roles, they increase their professionalism across campus. This fact is congruent with the move in some instances toward requiring campus officers to have college training and degrees. Many police academies are now requiring at least two years of college education. Requiring officers to achieve diversity skills would further enhance their continuing education and strengthen their integrity within the academic community. Certainly the law enforcement profession is an indirect beneficiary also.

Of course, there is a "down side" to increased professionalism. On many campuses, enforcement agencies are severely underpaid in comparison to their municipal counterparts (D. Rath, personal communication, April 1991). As the standards of education for the profession increase, salaries must grow accordingly; yet campus law enforcement salaries are inadequate now. Better educated and more culturally aware police officers will cost more to hire, retain, and promote. If diversity training enhances overall professionalism, departments may face even new dilemmas as they struggle to pay for these new professional talents.

Overtime Pay for Diversity Duties

Added to these other dilemmas is the reality that colleges must pay their officers to take on these new diversity roles. If an institution prizes diversity and wants to promote it, then should not officers be paid for their participation in the extra duties? If a campus police chief believes officers should attend minority student recruitment or retention functions or talk to minority parents about crime prevention on a Saturday morning, then officers should be paid for whatever overtime is incurred to achieve this diversity task. Officers receive overtime pay if they direct traffic at a Saturday football game or an evening rock concert if it falls outside their normal shift assignment. If the campus president believes it is important for an officer from the 11 p.m.-to-7 a.m. shift to attend a university-wide sexual assault task force meeting at 3 p.m., then the officer should be compensated for this activity just as he or she would be compensated for any other assigned service function. Again, financial and staffing resources can interfere with achieving diversity and enhancing the campus climate. To be sure, campus administrators and campus law enforcement personnel must collaborate to find solutions to these resource dilemmas which restrict officers' flexibility to participate in diversity activities.

Student Civilian Police Training

Attempting to increase positive interactions with the community and to better educate the public about their duties, municipal police departments have created civilian police training. In these eight- to ten-week training courses, civilians participate in such activities as learning basic police procedures, receiving firearm instruction, and riding with officers on actual patrols. This model is an easy one to duplicate within an educational environment where training and out-of-classroom learning is an everyday occurrence.

Student civilian campus police training is an excellent educational tool for all students. It can become an essential educational tool for diversity, used with such special populations as minority student organizations, gay and lesbian groups, student athletes, and others. By participating in this training, students learn about the law enforcement profession and have an opportunity to participate in real life activities which enhance their own living and learning environments. Such training serves also to enhance students' development of self-responsibility, autonomy, and self-reliance — all of which are important developmental tasks of college-age adults. Moreover, students will acquire other essential life tools, such as crime awareness and self-protection skills. The interaction with campus police would allow minority students, for example, to interact with adults about whom they know little. The student/staff interaction which would occur during a student civilian police academy is beneficial for all concerned, but the campus climate is the true beneficiary. Officers would learn about the developmental tasks of the "public" they serve, which will result in improved service to students. The officer/minority student interaction moves diversity a step further, in that the one-to-one interaction experienced in student training would help reduce the preconceptions and bias each holds about the other. The result of a student civilian police academy, if held over time, would be a closer relationship between students, especially minorities and other special population peers, and the campus police officers who educate and serve them.

The risks are few, but they are profound. Convincing students to commit to such training is a challenge. If college course credit were awarded for their participation, just as it is for other types of peer training activities, incentive to participate would increase. The problem of where to find the funds and the officers' time to create, deliver, and evaluate such a program will have to be resolved with the creative input from student affairs and business affairs staff, enhanced by a strong endorsement from faculty and college academic deans.

CONCLUSION

Enhancing the campus climate is an educational task whose responsibility falls upon campus law enforcement personnel and other educators equally. This chapter seeks to convince administrators, especially those within student affairs, that they must and should work with campus law enforcement professionals if campus-wide diversity is ever to be realized. Making certain that diversity is embraced requires that campus officers and student affairs staff first understand each other's unique roles in achieving this educational goal and then, together, assume collective leadership to support its growth across the entire campus.

Ensuring campus safety has been entrusted typically to campus law enforcement personnel — commissioned peace officers, security guards, and civilian staff who engage in a variety of law enforcement and service functions (Peak, 1989). Until officers are valued fully for their traditional roles, it will be hard for them to assume new, educational service roles. These future roles define their responsibility for the academic, personal, and social growth of students, at least as it relates to achieving diversity. By assuming this new responsibility, officers and their departments increase their status among campus professionals, faculty, administrators, and especially students.

Campus police officers have diversity roles in two pivotal areas. They can help students learn crime awareness and crime prevention skills, particularly when those crimes may have a racial, gender, or other cultural overtone. Officers can assume leadership by helping students and their organizations become educated about potential "crimes of bigotry and ignorance," teaching students — minority and nonminority, international and domestic — how to recognize the risk of such violence and how best to protect themselves and their organizations, thereby making the campus safe for all.

Expanding campus law enforcement departments' diversity roles on campus requires new strategies. Their potential as student development educators, as recruiters for minorities, and as policy planners are but a few of the new diversity roles open to law enforcement personnel. Clearly, if college administrators are seriously committed to enhancing the campus climate for diversity, then the alliance between campus law enforcement and student affairs educators is essential to confirming the university's commitment to diversity and having an open campus climate. If minorities, gays, lesbians, and the physically challenged each alter their impressions of police and if the police, in turn, change their impressions of students, then a large barrier is removed, opening doors to personal autonomy and expanding the freedom to learn for all.

References

American Council on Education (1988). *One third of a nation.* A report of the commission on minority participation in education and American life. Washington, D.C.: author.

Bess, W.R., and Horton, G.R. (1988). The role of campus law enforcement. *Campus Law Enforcement Journal,* 18(4), 35-44.

Esposito, D., and Stormer, D. (1989). The multiple roles of campus law enforcement. *Campus Law Enforcement Journal,* 19(3), 26-30.

Nichols, D. (1985). A study: The role perception conflict of campus public safety departments. *Campus Law Enforcement Journal,* 15(3), 5-7.

Nichols, D. (1987). *The administration of public safety in higher education.* Springfield, Illinois: Charles C. Thomas.

Peak, K. (1989). Campus law enforcement in flux: Changing times and future expectations. *Campus Law Enforcement Journal,* 19(6), 21-25.

CHAPTER FOUR

Enhancing Cultural Diversity and Building a Climate of Understanding
Becoming an Effective Change Agent

Suzanne E. Gordon
Connie Borders Strode

As issues of cultural diversity and multiculturalism impact on our campuses, institutions must develop systems and programs that will serve individual groups as well as the community at large. While such efforts on one campus may not transfer easily to another, information about activities on other campuses can influence thinking and decision making on our home campuses.

To that end, this chapter explores some of the ways institutions are meeting the challenges of providing support services and cocurricular activities for minority students while creating a shared community between minority and nonminority students. We examine systems, programs, and activities initiated on several diverse campuses in terms of a model for organizational change because such efforts are implemented with the intention of creating change within the institution. Our intent is to provide descriptive data that may generate ideas and discussion, a framework for understanding the process of change which is occurring on these campuses, and some evaluation of the change process itself.

CONCEPTUAL FRAMEWORK

The conceptual framework for this research is a model for organizational development presented by Hammons (1982) who noted that organizational development "deliberately interferes with the ordinary functioning of the organization in order to correct or modify an ineffective operation" (p. 18). His model identified four stages normally occurring in the development (or change) process and 12 intervention strategies suggested by French and Bell (1978):

Stage One: Awareness of the need for change. A problem is recognized or a state of imbalance is perceived. Either can result from "competition, growth, decline, changes in the environment, or . . . assessment of the organization's performance against future needs" (p. 15).

Stage Two: Diagnosis. Strengths and weaknesses are examined, the problem is defined, and causal forces are identified.

Stage Three: Action plans, strategies, and techniques. Interventions occur based on plans that have been designed to fit the situation. These may include any of the following:

- Diagnostic or fact-finding activities

- Team-building activities designed to improve the

operation of system teams

- Intergroup activities to improve the cooperation and effectiveness of interdependent groups

- Survey-feedback activities that focus on data gathered by survey and plans designed as responses to that data

- Education and training activities

- Structural interventions that change task, structural and technological subsystems (e.g., job enrichment, physical facility changes)

- Process consultation activities on the part of a consultant

- Third-party peacemaking activities to manage conflict

- Coaching and counseling activities to help individuals examine and modify their behavior

- Life and career planning activities

- Planning and goal-setting activities

Stage Four: Monitoring, evaluating, and stabilizing. After change strategies have been implemented, adjustments can be made based on observation and assessment of results.

This model served as the framework for interview questions as well as for analysis of printed materials as described below.

Research Method

During 1989 and 1990, several program sessions at both national and regional NASPA conferences reported on nationally recognized institutional efforts to enhance cultural diversity and multiculturalism. Knowing that these sessions had been selected because of their substance and quality, we identified institutions from this pool which had initiated exemplary systems, programs, and activities geared toward providing support for minority students and enhancing campus community. Because we wanted to provide in-depth descriptive data that would be of interest to the widest possible audience, we also limited the sample to six to ten institutions with diverse characteristics (see Table 1 below). Of the nine institutions contacted, seven chose to participate: Duke University, Iowa State University, Pennsylvania State University, Rockhurst College, the University of Cincinnati,

Table 1
Institutional Characteristics

Institution	NASPA Region	Type	Enrollment	% Diversity
Duke University	III	Private	10,370	15%
Iowa State University	IV-E	Public	25,490	5%
Pennsylvania State University	II	Public	37,720	9%
Rockhurst College	IV-W	Private	3,230	13%
University of Cincinnati	IV-E	Public	36,000	13%
University of Northern Colorado	IV-W	Public	10,240	9%
University of Wisconsin	IV-E	Public	10,270	6%

the University of Northern Colorado, and the University of Wisconsin-Whitewater.

In telephone interviews, senior-level student affairs officers at the institutions were queried about their institutions' moves toward multiculturalism: What created a need for change on their campus? What problems were identified? What strengths were identified? What action plans and strategies were agreed upon? We then analyzed mission statements and program materials to determine which, if any, of the previously mentioned intervention strategies were being used.

We concluded the study by asking representatives of two groups to comment on their perceptions of the effects of the institutional efforts to enhance multiculturalism. In telephone interviews, various institutions' presidents and small groups of student leaders (including student government presidents and leaders of minority organizations) were asked four questions: Has climate changed as a result of the programs? What has not changed that needs to? What would you do differently? What should be done next?

This approach to the research allowed us to present a distinctive view of effort and institutional commitment on each campus as expressed by not only published materials but also personal perceptions. Because each institution has a unique background and approach to the issues, we will review our findings as they relate to stages and specific intervention strategies at individual institutions before synthesizing the findings.

Research Findings
Duke University. Duke University in Durham, North Carolina, is a private institution affiliated with the United

Methodist Church. Of the 10,370 students, 6 percent is African American, 1 percent is Native American, 3 percent is Hispanic, and 5 percent is Asian American. Stage One, the awareness of the need for change, began in 1988 at Duke following complaints from an all-female residence hall that racist remarks were made in a hall meeting. To diagnose the problem, meetings and workshops were held with hall residents, questions were asked, and members of various cultural organizations were brought together with faculty and student affairs administrators.

Stages Two and Three began once people were talking about the issues. Plans and strategies were formulated that emerged as "Duke's Vision," and the support of the institution's president was sought. Now, as a result of monitoring and evaluation, the program has been expanded and materials and activities are being revised on the basis of feedback from students and faculty.

Specifically, the strategies used at Duke focused on articulating that institution's commitment to multiculturalism to all members of the community, with the emphasis on incoming freshmen. Duke's Vision is a cohesive package of strategies used prior to and during freshman orientation. During the summer, incoming students receive the booklet entitled *Duke's Vision*, which emphasizes the advantages of a multicultural campus and the issues raised in such an environment, along with a letter from President Keith Brodie urging students to consider these issues.

At orientation, students hear both President Brodie and Maya Angelou, a professor of American studies at Wake Forest University, discuss multiculturalism, then they break into living groups to participate in what is described as Duke's first exam. This exam is an inventory designed to reveal individual prejudices and provides a springboard for discussion led by selected faculty members. It is based on real-life experiences of the students who helped develop the vision program.

Because of interest expressed by resident advisors and freshman advisory counselors, who participated in workshops on multiculturalism so they can help with the program during orientation, Duke's Vision is now available to all students through programming in the residence halls.

Presidential support for Duke's Vision has come in the form of budget allotments and public communications, including a letter to freshmen and opening convocation addresses with multiculturalism as the theme. Students are involved in every piece of written material associated with the program, helping to write, revise, and edit. The program undoubtedly benefits from both types of involvement.

Iowa State University. Iowa State University is a regional institution in Ames, Iowa. Total enrollment is 25,490; 3 percent is African American, 1 percent is Hispanic, and 1 percent is Asian American. Consistent complaints about living in residence halls and problems between roommates of different ethnic backgrounds brought attention to the need for change at Iowa State University. In 1988, the Student Affairs Division brought in a consultant to diagnose the problem by reviewing and evaluating services the Department of Residence provided to ethnic minority students.

Stage Three interventions that added to or modified existing efforts were the result of that review and the recommendations made. The division is now in Stage Four, with an ongoing assessment of its programs, including regular student evaluations, meetings with students, and staff documentation of contacts with minority students.

Interventions were based on the consultant's recommendations. The first step was to fill the position of coordinator of residential minority programs which had been vacant for over a year. Minority student support groups are a major focus of the programming. They are formed in the residence halls for the various ethnic groups, and each targets a specific population. They are designed to improve the quality of life for minority students, and programming and printed information is available on minority involvement opportunities on campus.

To avoid exclusivity in these groups, staff are focusing on a multicultural environment, and a multicultural programming committee of both minority and nonminority students is being developed to identify issues and needs in the halls. In addition, a student affairs human relations committee helps to establish division goals and is responsible for multicultural programming for staff.

President Gordon Eaton has taken a proactive stance, challenging the university community to "identify and define these principles (of integrity, quality, and freedom) and to begin to work toward achieving them in a way that is obvious to all."

Pennsylvania State University. Pennsylvania State University is part of University Park Campus in State College, Pennsylvania. Of the 37,720 students, 4 percent is African American, 1 percent is Native American, 1 percent is Hispanic, and 3 percent is Asian American. An awareness of the need for change came quickly to Penn State and its community when, in 1987, racist stickers appeared on campus. Although they were removed immediately, the press condemned then-President Bryce Jordan for not making an immediate statement. Bypassing the diagnostic stage, the administration created the *Model for Managing Intolerance* within two weeks after the incident.

Intervention has been an ongoing process since that time, aimed at creating what one administrator calls "permeating change." To monitor progress, staff submit quarterly reports on what they do individually in their areas of responsibility to enhance diversity. A campus environment team, whose only purpose is to assess and make recommendations, meets weekly to review incidents at all 22 Penn State locations, to look for patterns in behavior, and to assess climate from a student's point of view. The team consists of the vice president and assistant vice president for campus life, the affirmative action officer, the assistant vice president for safety, a representative from the president's office, the vice provost for underrepresented groups, and a representative from the public relations office.

Intervention strategies at Penn State are extensive and cut across all groups within the institution as well as the surrounding communities. A "Log of Diversity-Related Activities at Penn State" is 29 pages long and lists activities involving student groups, central administration, community action, public pronouncements, and campus events during the 1989-90 academic year.

The *Model for Managing Intolerance* is the core document in efforts to enhance diversity. Its thrust is that response to incidents is not enough; rather, the institution needs to work in four areas simultaneously: improving climate, anticipating circumstances, preparing for quick (within hours) response, and assessing results. Programming that results from the model utilizes existing staff and resources, involves separate offices, and benefits from top-down advocacy since former president Jordan was the leader in its development.

Some of the more noteworthy strategies at Penn State included creation of the vice provost position to administer programs for all underrepresented groups; town/gown diversity workshops; advertisements promoting diversity and tolerance in the student newspaper; required freshman and family orientation on multiculturalism; and a comprehensive approach to investigating intolerance incidents and identifying and addressing individual, campus, and community needs following such incidents.

Presidential involvement in and support of efforts to enhance diversity is a highly visible and important factor in the programming at Penn State. The impact of diversity issues on this campus is also highly visible in articles and editorials in campus publications, posters, policy statements, residence hall special publications, and articles in local newspapers on the issues.

Rockhurst College. Rockhurst College, in Kansas City, Missouri, is an independent Roman Catholic institution. Of the 3,230 students, 9 percent is African American, 3 percent is Hispanic, and 1 percent is Asian American.

Awareness of the need to enhance cultural diversity at Rockhurst College has come primarily from a new president who has indicated the importance of being partners with the community and becoming more involved in society and the changing world. He has asked faculty and staff to confront change and has infused a new sense of creativity within the institution.

The diagnosis stage has not been coordinated but seems to be happening throughout the college. The student affairs division formed an African American student focus group which identified problems, such as feelings of isolation, few black role models, occasional racist comments, and curriculum not including information about African American scholars. Also, the Lilly Foundation funded a summer project for a faculty team to focus on cultural awareness — both what is happening as well as what needs to happen. Because interventions are fairly recent, the assessment stage has not begun.

Intervention strategies at Rockhurst have been varied in approach. A recent graduate was hired as a multicultural affairs specialist, and a session on multicultural affairs was implemented at new student orientation. A gift from a former faculty member provided funds for faculty development to infuse multicultural issues into the classroom. In addition, an African American alumni club was formed to help with recruitment efforts, and the college was closed for Martin Luther King's birthday. The student affairs division sponsored a half-day workshop for all student affairs' staff with the Lilly group to discuss multiculturalism. Perhaps most significant, recruitment initiatives have resulted in a 100 percent increase in minority students in the freshman class (from 8-9 percent to 17-18 percent).

University of Cincinnati. The University of Cincinnati is a state-supported regional institution. It is part of the University of Cincinnati System and is in downtown Cincinnati. Some 30,700 students, primarily from Ohio, are enrolled. Ten percent of the student body is African American, 1 percent is Hispanic, and 2 percent is Asian American.

Diversity has been a long-standing issue at the University of Cincinnati, which first admitted African American students in the 1960s and became a city university in the 1970s. It is located downtown where 40 percent of the residents are African Americans. An undercurrent of misunderstanding has existed between town and gown. A Board of Trustees which increasingly values diversity, the changing racial demographics of downtown Cincinnati, an increasing number of racial incidents, and a perception of some minority students that they are tolerated but not welcomed by the university community formed the basis for recognizing a need for change.

The University of Cincinnati appears to be moving simultaneously between Stages One, Two, Three, and Four. They continue to evaluate strengths and weaknesses and define problems that need to be solved, as well as develop actual plans and strategies. Overall results of institutional efforts are difficult to measure; however, individual programs and efforts are being monitored and assessed.

Several unique strategies or interventions are being implemented at the University of Cincinnati. In 1988, the president organized an Advisory Council on Race Relations and Human Decency with the intent of changing the campus climate. After a year of meetings and discussions, the council published its recommendations:

❏ create a cabinet-level affirmative action office

❏ establish a free speech and civility policy

❏ increase the number of minority faculty, staff, and students

❏ develop a curricula which reflects a multiethnic society

❏ emphasize racial and cultural programs

❏ redirect budgetary resources and set specific time frames to accomplish recommendations.

These recommendations were published and distributed university-wide, along with the president's commitment to hiring a director for the Office of Affirmative Action and a Board of Trustee's resolution supporting recent and future initiatives.

In September 1989, the Coordination Committee for Undergraduate Education composed of faculty and administrators published *Undergraduate Experience at the University of Cincinnati: Major Issues.* One of the major issues was a commitment to multicultural education in both the academic program and the out-of-classroom activities and to support services and a caring attitude toward students from other racial and ethnic backgrounds. To implement recommendations, the committee called for dialogue and discussion along with concrete initiatives and budget allocations.

Mary Ellen Ashley, vice provost for undergraduate and student affairs, developed a resource book and model for the 1990s entitled *Combatting Racism on Campus.* The model provided workbook material from which a department head or institution could conduct an analysis of commitment, climate, and accountability to measure efforts to respond effectively to racism on campus.

The Student Senate passed a bill requiring all members of student government to participate in a training program to increase their sensitivity and awareness regarding multicultural and multiracial issues. They also passed a bill encouraging all students to enroll in at least one African American studies course.

University of Northern Colorado. The University of Northern Colorado in Greeley, Colorado, has an enrollment of 9,650 students. It is a state-supported institution. Two percent of the student body is African American, 6 percent is Hispanic, and 1 percent is Asian America. Awareness of the need to enhance cultural diversity began in 1981 at the University of Northern Colorado with a new president, and in 1982 the Board of Trustees approved a commitment to diversity. Recently, the Colorado Commission for Higher Education mandated that 18.6 percent of the graduating class in the year 2000 must be minority. Yearly goals have been set and those institutions not meeting this goal will assume a 2 percent budget reduction.

The diagnosis state included program reviews and needs assessment. As a result, action plans throughout the university were developed, including establishment of a Center for African Americans in 1983, a Hispanic Center in 1984, and an International Student Cultural Center in 1985. Also, in 1984 the board strengthened the 1982 commitment with a new document that addressed the major topics of overall coordination, evaluations and reporting, employment procedures, recruitment and retention of students, cultural sensitivity, academic programs, and dissemination of reports and analysis.

After nearly 10 years, Stage Four is now proceeding. An institutional objective for the 1990-91 academic year was to review and publish the university's progress and to set new goals and objectives for the future.

Numerous intervention strategies have been implemented throughout the student affairs division; however, efforts in recruiting and retaining minority students are perhaps most outstanding. Such strategies include outreach and specific partnership programs with secondary schools, community colleges, and community organizations; telephone and home visit programs; and follow-up letters to perspective students and parents from admissions personnel, directors of the various cultural centers on campus, and freshman mentors (faculty, staff, and students).

In other efforts, annual workshops for supervisory employees are conducted to enhance cultural sensitivity; the Dean's Council was directed to submit a plan to raise the social and ethnic awareness of faculty and staff; a professional conduct code was developed; and a grievance system to resolve discriminatory and sexual harassment complaints was implemented.

University of Wisconsin-Whitewater. The University of Wisconsin-Whitewater is a state-supported comprehensive institution. It is part of the University of Wisconsin System. The university is in a small town with easy access to Milwaukee. Of the 10,270 students, 3 percent is African American, 1 percent is Native American, 1 percent is Hispanic, and 1 percent is Asian American.

Their awareness and recognition of the problem was propelled forward with the university system president Kenneth A. Shaw's Design for Diversity which presented a comprehensive system strategy for increased diversity on campuses (see Chapter 6). Institutional support for the design includes "top level responsibility, measurable accountability, and the authority and resources sufficient to achieve success."

The diagnosis and action stages consisted of a study of the racial environment at the University of Wisconsin-Whitewater and a resulting plan of action. Shaw's design required the chancellor to submit a report on institutional problems and how they could be addressed, accountability, and timelines for each year of the plan. Subsequently, the Student Affairs Division submitted a document to address the six goals of the overall diversity plan:

❏ educate all students for an increasingly multicultural society

❏ improve recruiting and retention efforts

❏ complete evaluation of recruiting and retention efforts

❏ remove financial barriers for minorities and economically disadvantaged

❏ increase the number of minority staff

❏ establish effective partnerships with public schools, the community, and private sector.

Stage Four has resulted in various instruments being developed within the departments to assess progress and effectiveness, a research position being filled for the division, and focus groups and informal contacts with students being established.

Structural interventions have been used on the University of Wisconsin-Whitewater campus. Both the chancellor's office and the Student Affairs Division hired individuals to monitor daily progress of the plan, up to $100,000 was designated for developing programs to improve the campus multicultural environment, and a mission statement for the Student Affairs Division was adopted which accepted responsibility for developing a campus environment that designs, encourages, and celebrates diversity.

An intergroup strategy has been implemented — a race relations training team — to educate student organizations and staff in race relations and multiculturalism. In addition, a multicultural retreat has been expanded beyond student leaders to include faculty and staff, and members of the academic community participate in planning and implementing student/staff exchange programs between Grambling University and the University of Wisconsin-Whitewater.

Some strategies aim to retain minority staff: funding and release time to pursue advanced degrees; development grants to enhance employability; "career ladders" (such as internships, mentor programs, and position exchanges) within the university to provide promotion opportunities; and longitudinal studies which identify factors that contribute to or detract from minority staff retention.

DISCUSSION

It is natural that each institution's story is different and that the interventions used are different in tone and texture. But commonalities also exist that begin to point the way for other institutions. In looking at these similarities, we will return to our conceptual framework.

While progression through the stages identified by Hammons (1982) is unique to each campus, there are some similarities that suggest that this developmental model presents a natural process for the changes that occur when institutions attempt to enhance multiculturalism.

How Change Was Instituted

Stage One awareness came to these campuses from one of two directions: president and boards committed to diversity or students voiced the need for wrongs to be addressed. Stage Two diagnosis involved, for most, studies, program reviews, needs assessments, and internal/external consultation. Stage

Three strategies are discussed below. Stage Four is an ongoing process of assessment, revision, and expansion that is leading to overall reviews of progress.

The use of specific strategies at these institutions is particularly interesting when viewed in terms of French and Bell's (1978) typology. Fifty percent of the strategies used fell evenly into the two categories of Education/Training and Structural/Subsystem interventions. The first would be anticipated at an educational institution, but the second is particularly noteworthy because such strategies represent a concrete, long-term commitment to change on the part of the governing structure.

Structural/Subsystem interventions involved changes in budgeting and hiring practices as well as additions to and changes in the curriculum. New administrative and staff positions along with special offices were created, and expanded lines of communication were opened. Changes were made in policies and codes as well as statements of mission and goals. Models were created for whole institutions to follow. Such strategies accounted for 25 percent of the changes made on the seven campuses.

The variety of education and training strategies used reflects the expertise of higher education institutions in creating programs to achieve educational ends. The particulars are too numerous to list, but board categories include cultural sensitivity and race relations workshops, multicultural retreats, conferences, courses, and publications. These strategies also composed 25 percent of those used.

Another 25 percent of the interventions were grouped evenly into more types: Intergroup and Coaching/Counseling. These, like Education/Training, also seem particularly suited to a higher education setting.

To promote interaction among various groups on and off campus, various strategies were used. Faculty served as discussion leaders for students at workshops designed by student affairs leaders. Retreats were designed to involve all segments of the population, and cross-cultural programming was instituted. Resource materials and programming ideas were shared by various groups, and departments reviewed reports from other departments. Occasionally programming extended beyond the campus into the community.

Coaching/Counseling strategies in many cases began with top-down communications from institution presidents who urged the importance of multicultural issues. Orientation programs, support groups, mentor programs, and discussion groups enhanced educational programs. Special publications and conflict resolution techniques promoted understanding among diverse groups.

The strategies least used were those that would be categorized as Survey Feedback and Planning/Goal Setting. While the first would seem to be an appropriate way to gather information from which to develop programs, such action only occurred on two campuses. However, as the evaluation stage progresses, use of survey instruments may increase. Planning/Goal Setting strategies undoubtedly underlie the use of the types of strategies and so may not be seen as separate intervention.

As these patterns of strategies for enhancing diversity began to emerge, one is prompted to ask: How successful have they been? While each institution is assessing its own programs, we wanted reactions of those not in the formal evaluation process. To this end, several institution presidents as well as student leaders on several campuses were interviewed.

Perceptions of Change

The effects of these stages and interventions on the institution were viewed by chief executive officers in the following ways. Presidents reported the primary change on their campuses has been an increased number of minority faculty, staff, and students. Although more difficult to document, they also felt that a more positive environment had been created. To a greater extent, minority students feel wanted and supported. In addition, more nonminority students are participating in joint activities.

Although recognizing some changes, two of the presidents indicated they were just beginning to implement programs. More needed to be done with faculty and students who were not blatantly racist, but who definitely needed their consciences raised. Another president stressed the need for changes in the community where many doors were closed to minorities.

In looking back, several presidents stated they would have started their cultural diversity campaigns earlier with a more focused and coordinated approach. One president believed that change on a college campus must be gradual. He reported that a former president had begun opening up the campus and he, as a new president of two years, had developed a strategic plan with targets and dates. This building process allowed for developmental growth and a grassroots acceptance to continue the momentum. Another president recognized that discretionary funding would have moved the process along more speedily.

Changes that still needed to be accomplished included a continued increase in the number of minorities at the various campuses, adding multiculturalism issues in the curriculum, and developing creative ways to attract and retain minorities.

Several presidents added that this was not a success story, only a progress report. One president indicated that although several governmental agencies were not supportive of certain diversity issues and affirmative action, this was not going to deter the efforts on his campus. He hoped that faculty and staff would continue to move forward, but if they choose not to, then they should not stand in the way of progress.

Students, too, believed that change is necessary but gradual. When asked whether things had changed on their campuses as a result of multicultural programming, student leaders agreed that there was evidence of change, but it was slow and intermittent. However, they did not seem discouraged by this; they felt that changing attitudes takes time, "like turning around the Queen Elizabeth," as one put it. They noted that the tendency is for only a handful of students to get involved in the programs, but that the number is growing and once people get involved in one aspect they are likely to get involved in others.

The main change students noticed was a change in sensitivity and understanding of the issues. People are becoming more aware of the impact of remarks that demean and stereotype; tokenism is fading as understanding spreads. Administration and faculty are actively involved in spreading awareness. Such changes are significant in what one student termed "a never-ending struggle."

However, some things have not changed as much as the students felt they needed to. More acknowledgement of multicultural issues needs to be reflected in the classroom as well as in curricular requirements. A single course requirement or limited classroom references restrict students' ability to understand the wide range of cultures functioning in the modern world. This concern broadens into an overall perception that all facets of the university — administration, faculty, staff, and students — must be involved and committed to diversity.

Despite increasing sensitivity to the issues, student leaders note that too much insensitivity still exists. They attribute some of it to people who believe that any programming is enough and to a lack of focus on the causes of intolerant incidents.

They suggest that some things need to be done differently. More minority faculty to serve as role models are needed. The concern implicit in voluntary physical separation of races on campuses needs to be addressed. Diverse ethnic organizations need to band together to have more impact, and the work of these groups needs to be strongly supported with recognition as well as funding. In addition, some feel that multicultural programming should be obligatory for all members of the campus community and should be broadened to include civic communities of which campuses are part.

In looking forward to future action, student leaders responded simply, "Continue to question and be aware; involve more people; recognize the contributions and advances that are being made."

RECOMMENDATIONS

As a result of the analysis of interviews and documents, we present the following recommendations for becoming an effective agent for change. Some may appear to be self-evident; nevertheless, they were an important part of the data in this study.

Promote campus-wide commitment. The commitment of everyone, from president and boards to line and staff people to faculty to students, is needed to make the changes that can affect behaviors and then attitudes.

Increase awareness of issues. All segments of the community should be exposed to multicultural issues through publications, lectures, meetings, programs, and extensive formal and informal interaction.

Modify behavior. Appropriate and acceptable behavior should be defined and this definition widely disseminated.

Advocate structural change. The institution should model behavior through structural changes that affect not only policies and procedures but also organization makeup, communication channels, and financial priorities. Such changes reflect the institution's strong commitment to create lasting change.

Personify individual commitment. Commitment from those in the position to mandate and institute such changes may not be forthcoming. Nevertheless, individual, personal commitments have been and can be made by those who are in a position to influence both other administrators and students — student affairs professionals.

Model personal behaviors that foster diversity (patience, persistence, and risk taking). Patience is needed for, as both presidents and students pointed out, the process of changing attitudes is a gradual one. Persistence is required because the changes must be made for the higher education community to remain viable in today's world. But patience and persistence will not suffice if individuals and communities are not willing to take the risks involved in building bridges between cultures.

Student affairs professionals can reflect such behaviors by being diverse in their activities, from hiring practices to social engagements, and be willing to take a stand for the issues when the opportunity arises. This commitment to diversity is also evidenced by those who give themselves and others credit for any impact or change that is made, however small.

But perhaps the most effective thing a student affairs professional can do is spread the word that diversity in the community is an important issue. Giving others access to information such as that contained in this monograph, then being willing to discuss the issues, can in time allow a community to begin the process for change.

References

French, W.L., and Bell, C.H., Jr. (1978). *Organization development: Behavioral science interventions for organization improvement.* Englewood Cliffs, N.J.: Prentice-Hall.

Hammons, J.O. (1982). Organization development: An overview. In J.O. Hammons (Ed.), *Organization development: Change strategies.* San Francisco: Jossey-Bass.

CHAPTER FIVE

The Making of a Celebration
Lessons From University of Louisville's First University-Wide Celebration of Diversity

Dennis C. Golden
John I. Gilderbloom
Victoria L. Guthrie

The predominant issue in American higher education in the 1990s is diversity. One of the most important aspects of the education of our students, and yet often the most neglected, is that of developing informed, accepting, and tolerant attitudes within a community in which diversity is valued and differences are embraced. As we enter the '90s "many more

The authors gratefully acknowledge the contributions of Phyllis Webb, Linda Wilson, Denise Fitzpatrick, Adam Mathery, Patricia Gilderbloom, and Jim Van Fleet. Special assistance and funding for this project was contributed by Donald C. Swain, president of the University of Louisville. Additionally, Ralph Fitzpatrick, director of the Office of Minority Services, is recognized for his leadership, cooperation, and support. Finally, we acknowledge the contributions of the following graduate students who participated in the research study institutions are beginning to articulate a commitment to educate students for living in a pluralistic world and to create environments that embrace diversity" (Fleming, 1990).

The term *diversity* incorporates men and women; young and old; abled and disabled; straight and gay; African American and European American; Asian and Hispanic; Native American and Arabic; along with other cultures, ethnic groups, and religions. It is increasingly used to describe the makeup of today's student body which is significantly more heterogeneous than higher education has ever seen.

Valuing diversity means recognizing that individuals are different and that differences are to everyone's advantage if they are accepted, understood, valued, nurtured, and utilized. Valuing diversity also means changing behavior and systems to nurture the richness of these differences. According to Ravitch (1990), ". . . the unique feature of the U.S. is that its common culture has been formed by the interaction of its subsidiary cultures . . . American music, art, literature, language, food, clothing, sports, holidays, and customs all show the effects of the commingling of diverse cultures into one nation" (p. 339).

The Carnegie Foundation for the Advancement of Teaching (1990) stated there were six principles that define the kind of community every college and university should

and prepared preliminary reports of the findings: William P. Friedlander, Gary Dennis, Mary Henderson, Gracie Wishnia, Greg Bucholtz, Samantha Israel, David A. Collins, Mike Burayidi, Sheila Thompson, Pat Bailey, Dennis J. Golden, David W. Parrot, Karen King, Manuel McMillan, Mark Buchter, Stephen L. Wagner, and Frances Campeau.

strive to be. Each also has implications for meeting the challenge of diversity:

❐ Creation of a purposeful community involves building "creative, intellectual and social unity" through all college events cutting across departmental interests which "can be especially valuable in stirring a common intellectual purpose on the campus" (p. 13).

❐ An open community is one in which "a climate of reasoned discourse is established . . . and civility is powerfully affirmed" (p. 17).

❐ A just community is "a place where the sacredness of each person is honored and where diversity is aggressively pursued . . . Higher education builds community out of the rich resources of its members. It rejects prejudicial judgments, celebrates diversity, and seeks to serve the full range of citizens in our society effectively" (p. 25).

❐ A disciplined community is a place where individuals know and accept their "obligations to the group" and where behavior is guided "for the common good" (p. 46).

❐ The campus should be a caring community, a place where "the well-being of each member is sensitively supported and . . . where every individual feels affirmed" (p. 47).

❐ In a celebrative community "rituals affirming both tradition and change are widely shared" (p. 8).

"In that same spirit colleges and universities should schedule special events throughout the year that highlight the

rich contributions of the racial and ethnic groups on campus"
to demonstrate that "culturally diverse perspectives are an
essential part of what everyone in the community needs to
know" (p. 61).

CELEBRATION OF DIVERSITY PROGRAM

The Carnegie Foundation's (1990) principles served as a
cornerstone for the University of Louisville's first annual
university-wide Celebration of Diversity Program. This was
a ten-day program for the university, featuring educational,
inspirational, and social activities emphasizing cultural,
ethnic, and racial diversity themes. As an urban university
with an enrollment of 23,000, the University of Louisville
incorporates many diverse populations within the student
body.

The University of Louisville had experienced racial
incidents and the moment was right to emphasize issues of
diversity. Racial incidents cited on the campus included but
were not limited to: residence hall conflicts, classroom
problems, racial slurs, graffiti markings, and the need for
revisions in the curriculum. The charge for a Celebration of
Diversity Program began with the university president and
resulted in an institutional commitment that extended from
the Board of Trustees through the faculty and administration
to the student body.   The Celebration of Diversity was
designed to be proactive through education and the
celebration of differences as opposed to a reactive or negative
response.

Perhaps the most vital element of the celebration was the
institution realizing this effort required sustained
commitment rather than episodic interest (Smith, 1989).

From the outset all involved recognized that this program represented only a part of the total institutional response to the issue of diversity. Yet, because of its magnitude, it would serve as a significant step and make a positive statement to the university community about the university's values and commitments.

The fact that the celebration would bring criticism and significant risk was understood and accepted early on. The president himself said he expected that "sparks would certainly fly" but that this was in keeping with the nature of a free and open university. The prophesy of inevitable risks and sparks came true. A radical African American leader complained to the press that the Celebration of Diversity was a "joke" and failed to present an exclusively Afrocentric perspective. A conservative white faculty member felt the program might be divisive. One particular issue that generated much debate was whether an Asian American should be a featured speaker. Criticism came from both internal and external sources; there was pressure about philosophy, skepticism of speakers, debates about dates, criticisms of costs, and misrepresentations of motivations. However, the greater the stress, the greater became the strength to do the right thing.

The President
Unless the president of the institution makes a commitment, you cannot and will not be successful in enhancing diversity (Green, 1989; Washington & Harvey, 1989). University of Louisville President Donald C. Swain officially notified the provost, the eleven deans, the vice presidents, and his entire staff that they were personally and professionally responsible for enhancing diversity within their assigned areas. President

Swain incorporated this mandate in his annual *Five-Year Strategic Directions Document,* his operation plan; and all involved have adopted similar principles in their unit plans and their priorities for action. In addition, President Swain initiated a special faculty recruitment and retention program for African American faculty, and he has funded it accordingly. President Swain issued his charge letter for the celebration on April 20, 1990. The principle parts of the letter to the vice president for student affairs and task force members read as follows:

> Accordingly, the University of Louisville must encourage
> harmonious relations and better understanding among diverse racial
> and cultural groups. We need to generate greater appreciation for
> the richness of pluralism. We ought to "celebrate diversity" in a
> positive, deliberate way . . . These events could include such things
> as special lectures by distinguished speakers, a University-wide
> convocation, special games and contests in which diverse racial and
> cultural groups participate together, a film festival, social
> occasions, academic events, etc. Please unleash your imaginations.

Task Force Issues
With the charge articulated, the task force members realized more than ever before that addressing diversity would be a complex and challenging mission. At a minimum it would require care, concern, conviction, and courage. At the maximum, it would have people who were fully committed to being change agents. As Smith (1989) pointed out in meeting the challenge of diversity, leadership plays a central role — not only in the setting of goals and provision of resources, but also in framing the questions and setting the tone for deliberations.

What the planners of the Celebration of Diversity discovered was that this leadership role was unlike any other they had experienced. Dealing with diversity is both formidable and fragile. It is something that cannot be read about from a book. It must be wanted, felt, loved, believed, and eventually owned. And, to do it well, one must intensely and passionately involve his or her value system, beliefs, mind, heart, spirit and will.

At the University of Louisville, traditional management principles were abandoned in favor of a servant-leadership model which was the basis for the enormous trust within the task force. A sincere belief in and frequent expression of this trust and evidence of professional pride was the social cement that held the group together.

The celebration was planned and implemented by a combined student, faculty, administrative committee in accordance with the president's charge letter which had been issued five months earlier. The effort was coordinated under the leadership of the vice president for student affairs who chaired the committee and the director of the Office of Minority Services who served as vice chair. The initial committee of nine was expanded to approximately 17 because as the work progressed, increased input, representation, and person power were needed to properly plan, coordinate, and implement a program of this breadth and consequence.

Specific tasks included having the right people contact the speakers, negotiate the contracts, organize the logistics, keep the time and place documents, communicate with campus and community constituencies, confer with the media, outreach to the faculty, secure the support of the minority groups, conduct evaluations, and write and publish program brochures. Task force members were implored to "think big" and the chair was ready to intervene when certain tasks were not being implemented.

Everyone involved with the planning understood the need to celebrate diversity and the possible backlash against such celebrations. Committee members were committed to expansion as opposed to constriction, inclusivity as opposed to exclusivity, and genuine progress as opposed to regression and fraudulent charades.

Program Description

For ten days during the early fall of 1990, the University of Louisville campus went from business as usual to a whirlwind of activity focusing on diversity. The Celebration of Diversity Program offered over 35 events as an exploration of cultural and racial values and traditions. The purpose of the program was to promote human dignity, tolerance, and appreciation for diversity.

Events included more than 20 lectures and various workshops, forums, films, discussions, entertainment events, and social programs specifically designed to meet the president's goals of "increasing awareness and appreciation for the different races and ethnic groups represented on the University campus." The speakers included some of the nation's leading spokespersons on cultural diversity:

> ❏ Derrick Bell, Jr., one of the nation's leading experts in civil
> rights law. Attorney Bell, a professor of law at Harvard University,
> served as dean of the University of Oregon School of Law, staff
> attorney to the NAACP Legal Defense Fund, and deputy assistant
> secretary for civil rights of the U.S. Department of Health,
> Education, and Welfare. His demand for more tenured African

American female law professors at Harvard led to recent front-page news stories around the country.

❏ Harry Edwards, a prominent sociologist at the University of California at Berkeley, social critic, author, and activist. Harry Edwards is the author of such books as *The Revolt of the Black Athlete; Black Students; The Sociology of Sports, The Struggle That Must Be;* and *Playing to Win: A Short Guide to Sensible Black Sports Participation.* He has been appointed distinguished scholar at 35 different universities. He is in the forefront of the movement to increase African American participation in coaching, management, and ownership of professional sports teams. He is also special advisor to the commissioner of major league baseball.

❏ Jamie Escalante, the East Los Angeles barrio calculus teacher who was immortalized in the film "Stand and Deliver." President Bush has declared Escalante his ideal of an American hero. A recent book on Escalante by Jay Matthews of the *Washington Post* calls him "the best teacher in America." Escalante's minority students rank near the top in the nation in mathematics test scores.

❏ Jacqueline Fleming, an expert on how personality sparks individual motivation differences. Fleming teaches undergraduate courses on the psychology of racism and human motivation at Barnard College where she is an adjunct professor. Her book, *Blacks in College*, suggests strategies that will provide an atmosphere that encourages African American students' fullest intellectual and personal growth. She also serves on the Advisory Committee of the United Negro College Fund.

❏ Edwin J. Nichols, a psychologist recently retired from the National Institute of Mental Health where he held various

positions, including section chief, Special Populations, and chief of
the Center for Studies of Child and Family Mental Health.

❐ Michael Woo, the first Asian American to serve on the Los
Angeles City Council. He is a leader of ethics reform and
represents an unusually diverse constituency of 198,000 people
who speak 54 separate languages and dialects. He is considered a
leading spokesperson for Asian American needs and rights in the
United States.

❐ Giancarlo Esposito, an actor and screenwriter. Esposito is best
known for his recent role as Bugging Out in Spike Lee's "Do The
Right Thing." The winner of an OBIE and the Theater World
Award, Esposito also appeared in the movies "School Daze,"
"King of New York," "Presumed Innocent," and "Mo' Better
Blues."

Topics dealt with by the speakers varied from
entertainment, gender, hiring practices, and athletics to
politics and education. These issues generated much
discussion among the participants during and after the
lectures.

In addition to the major lecture series, workshops
encouraged more in-depth discussion of issues relating to race
and cultural diversity. The films presented were portrayals of
minority life which were designed to sensitize individuals on
racial and cultural issues. Among the movies shown were
"Do the Right Thing," "Leadbelly," "My Left Foot," "El
Norte," and "Stand and Deliver." Social events included a
football half-time show that recognized the diversity theme,
an ethnic heritage festival, performance by the Black

Diamond Gospel Choir, an interfaith celebration, and Jamaican reggae dancers.

Diversity Logo
To establish and maintain a unified focus, a symbol is needed. The symbol used at the University of Louisville was the Covenant of Justice, Equity, and Harmony which originated with the Council of Churches in Boston, Massachusetts, during the late 1970s at a time of enormous tension and strife.

The Covenant of Justice, Equity, and Harmony logo consisted of an olive branch, the universal sign of peace and harmony; a red background, a symbol of the blood relationship that exists between and among people; a green branch, a sign of hope and the common dignity we share as human beings; and multicolored leaves, symbolizing the major races of people.

At the University of Louisville, the Student Government Association (SGA) president, Holly Everett, and the SGA Senate purchased thousands of T-shirts with the inscription "Celebrate Diversity" and the multicultural logo on the front center of the shirt. Huge banners with the symbol were placed on the academic buildings and in front of the new Student Activities Center. The covenant symbol was also printed on book markers and distributed throughout the campus. In addition, thousands of covenant buttons were distributed and people proudly wore them around campus and are still doing so months after the actual celebration. In sum, the goal was to establish a diversity symbol, adopt it, maintain momentum, and to proudly display the symbol as a statement of unity, care and concern.

When the University of Louisville football team played in the 1991 Fiesta Bowl, the diversity symbol was proudly worn by the coach, the players, band, cheerleaders, and thousands of fans at Sun Devil Stadium in Tempe, Arizona. This statement of commitment to diversity, in conjunction with honoring the legacy of Martin Luther King, Jr., was seen by millions of television viewers on New Years Day 1991. As the theme so proudly proclaimed, "The Dream Lives On."

Costs

A celebration of this kind is not cheap — nor should it be. But seldom if ever is there a line item budget for diversity. It is not necessary, nor preferable, to get first-rank guest speakers to your campus. However, at the University of Louisville we thought this was the best thing to do in 1990. The committee opted for recognized spokespersons as opposed to popular entertainers with speaker costs ranging from zero to $4,000 and an average cost of $2,500.

Essentially, the funding came from the offices of the president and the chief student affairs officer. In both cases, it meant that other things would go undone during 1991-92, but the unified leadership decision was to commit to the Celebration of Diversity. The combined cost for the entire program was close to $40,000. There has been much discussion and, at times, anger expressed because of this commitment, but it was a major step forward.

The celebration challenged the university to continue to move forward on diversity. As positive as the results are from the evaluation of the 1990 Celebration of Diversity Program, it was only a beginning in the minds of many respondents. In December of 1990, the Office of Student Affairs and the Urban Research Institute (URI) proposed a three-year one-half million dollar diversity program for the University of Louisville. This grant proposal will allow the university community in conjunction with the city of Louisville to continue to explore and work toward a more harmonious, tolerant, and respectful environment. It is hoped three years of funding for this program will establish a sound foundation of support which will allow us to realistically measure the degree of change in people's attitudes and the impact on enhancing our appreciation for diversity. The cost in dollars will be cheap; the return in harmony and understanding will be priceless.

Funding Sources for Diversity Programs
The Celebration of Diversity took a sizable commitment from the university of budget monies, staff time, and resources in the planning and implementing the ten-day program. Some important decisions were made in setting the agenda of addressing diversity as a priority for allocating this amount of funding. However, it is important to also realize that in these times of tight finances and budget cutbacks not only can this program be adapted in a less costly manner, but there are also alternative funding sources that can be explored.

First, funding can be sought from the student government association, student programming boards, and other campus speaker funds. There are often departmental speaker funds or faculty lecture series budgets that can also be tapped to create a combined, cosponsored effort. In some instances these funds go unutilized or the programs suffer due to lack of experience and sophistication in selecting a speaker, advertising, media relations, timing, and location. Coordinating these groups under one umbrella can provide a better focus and a sharing of talent in organizing a celebration. Student government in particular can play a pivotal role in linking together various organizations and developing a program that is representative of their respective needs.

A second source of funding is local or national foundations concerned with race relations and other issues of diversity. Working with the campus foundation specialist can yield a list of potential grants to pursue. Increasing numbers of organizations are listing diversity programs as a topic area for funding. However, grant writing is competitive and requires strong writing and research skills. Working together with faculty members with strong records of grant writing and demonstrated concern with diversity issues, grant proposals can be developed and external sources of funding can be tapped.

Another possible source of funding is city government. Community development block grant funds, human relations commission, and minority affairs offices in city government are potential sponsors of diversity programming on the campus — especially if the events are to be open to the community. Like foundations, these city agencies will likely require a detailed grant proposal.

Finally, the institutional budget can be carefully scrutinized for unutilized or underutilized pockets of funding that might be dedicated toward addressing the issue of diversity on campus. A major recommendation that came out of the Celebration of Diversity Program was to commit every dean to funding an annual lecture by a respected minority spokesperson and encourage greater faculty involvement.

Media Coverage
Celebration speakers Giancarlo Esposito and Michael Woo, President Donald Swain, and Holly Everett and Valerie

Ponder of the University of Louisville's Student Government Association fielded questions about racial and cultural diversity on "Metz Here," a radio call-in show that aired September 11 on WHAS-AM. The show has millions of listeners in 40 states.

Reporters from *The Courier-Journal, The Louisville Defender,* WHAS-TV, WAVE-TV, WLKY-TV, WDRB-TV, and WHAS-AM came to the September 12 news briefing. *The Courier-Journal* did four separate articles on the celebration. WLKY-TV did a noon live shot on the celebration, and WAVE-TV did live shots at noon and 5:00 p.m. WDRB-TV followed with a report on its 10:00 p.m. newscast, and WHAS-TV carried the story at 11:00 p.m.

Other stories appeared in *Inside U of L,* the university's faculty-staff newspaper; *The Louisville Cardinal,* University of Louisville's student newspaper; *The Louisville Defender*; and *Inside the Tureet,* a Fort Knox weekly. A taped interview with Giancarlo Esposito aired September 22 on "Closer Look," a public affairs program on WAVE-TV. Finally, the celebration received positive media coverage in the September 25 edition of *USA Today.*

Kentucky's largest newspaper, *The Courier-Journal,* declared in an editorial: "University of Louisville aimed to get racial concerns on the table with a celebration of diversity. Its success has been dramatic, albeit painful" ("A Bowlful of Opportunity," 1990).

Evaluation

An essential component of the Celebration of Diversity Program was the evaluation of its results. John Gilderbloom, a faculty member who served on the task force, directed a joint research effort combining the resources of administration with personnel from a graduate research methods course in the College of Urban and Public Affairs. The research proved to be invaluable in framing the success of the program and responding to its detractors. Although the scope of this chapter does not permit a full description of the methodology and reporting of the results, a brief summary follows. (A full report is available from the vice president for student affairs office.)

The study examined attitudes and reactions to the Celebration of Diversity Program. It was conducted by 18 graduate students. The method was based on teamwork, a primary component of which was the organization of tasks and division of labor. Steps in the process included developing the instrument, developing a sampling procedure, conducting the survey research, data processing and analysis, and interpreting and presenting the results.

A questionnaire including a mixture of open-ended and forced-choice items was administered to 220 randomly selected Celebration of Diversity participants by telephone. Nine major lectures were targeted from which to gather data. The response rate was 70 percent which is considered excellent. However, because the study was not conducted using a control group design, generalizations to the University of Louisville community as a whole or the general population based upon these results are not appropriate. It should also be recognized that participants attending the program may differ substantially from those choosing not to attend.

The results showed the Celebration of Diversity to be widely perceived as a timely, educational, and relevant program representing a positive step by the university administration toward creating greater understanding and acceptance of the diverse populations making up the university community.

The central message of the Celebration of Diversity Program was characterized by interviewees as follows: "Everyone needs to make an effort to know and understand each other." "Differences are something to celebrate . . . they are positive and not negative!" "The University is willing to deal with the issues of race . . . and will deal with it now before it becomes a problem." "We should respect other ethnic groups because everyone is different and everyone has something to contribute." "We need to get out and learn about other people and other ways of life." ". . . We should evaluate people by what is on the inside and not on the outside." And finally, "The university is committed to being an environment which recognizes and honors difference."

Program participants responded exceedingly well to the speakers with 98 percent giving a positive overall rating to the nine experts who were invited to speak. Perhaps the most encouraging finding was that over half of the participants surveyed indicated that they had been moved to make positive changes in their attitudes and behavior as a result of the program. For a faculty member the program "increased my fervor to help my students be more open and more tolerant." For another, it provided "concrete ideas for restructuring courses and curriculum. I was ready to make changes . . . now I have the information." A student remarked that the program caused him to "reevaluate myself and become more conscious of racial prejudices I have." And perhaps most to the point, "I will be more understanding of different cultures. I won't label people."

Through the survey, the university was challenged to continue and move forward. As positive as the results are, the Celebration of Diversity is only a beginning in the minds of many respondents. As one member of the university community stated, "It's not enough to say that we're going to have a week-long celebration — we must continue to explore and work toward respect for one another." However, interviewee after interviewee expressed praise and appreciation to the University of Louisville for taking "a lead in the community by addressing the issues of diversity" and "taking steps to make a change." While there was skepticism expressed by some — "I think this is a passing phase; one week, a lot of noise, and then it will pass" — others were looking to the future, ". . . this is not an answer, only a beginning. This is the frosting but the cake has yet to be baked."

Outcomes

The University of Louisville will never be the same because of the "power surge" that was put into the lifeline campus-wide. The faculty, administrators, and staff are more sensitive to and concerned about the principles and practical application of diversity.

While we are able to demonstrate empirically that greater sensitivity to minority needs has been realized, other positive outcomes can be attributed in part to the Celebration of Diversity Program, such as:

❏ greater scholarship aid

❏ mandate for annual Celebration of Diversity programs

❏ administrative expectations to include diversity issues in the curriculum

❏ more aggressive hiring of minority faculty and staff

❒ the director of the Office of Minority Services has more help in dealing with all student populations with particular emphasis on the African American students

❒ the university-wide enrollment management plan will be strengthened, both with recruiting and retention efforts for all needy and underprivileged students

❒ the athletic department has enhanced its involvement with the academic welfare of the student-athletes

❒ the concept of campus community (particularly for students) both inside and outside of class is becoming more of a reality

❒ the essence of racism, both direct and indirect, is being challenged frequently and effectively

❒ the 1991 Fiesta Bowl team displayed the diversity symbol to millions of viewers, as they honored the legacy of Martin Luther King, Jr.

❒ there will be ongoing research to analyze and foster more creative and teachable moments in a timely and helpful manner

❒ a Center for Cultural Diversity was established

SUMMARY

This chapter began with the argument that the most important issue in American higher education is diversity. This could also well be true for the survival of America as a nation because our country has so much possibility and responsibility regarding diversity.

Diversity should not be narrowly defined when one is attempting to ameliorate the insidious effects of long-term racial, cultural, and religious prejudice. Diversity themes should try to include African Americans, Hispanics, Asians, Native Americans, gender, and sexual orientation. This is a tall order and it is hard work, yet that is exactly why it is so important. Essentially stated, the theme of diversity is humanistic in tone imploring people not to judge each other by physical characteristics, culture, or value differences, but rather to acknowledge, understand, accept, enhance, and celebrate their diversity because of the unlimited possibilities involved.

A concise summary of what must happen to heighten the possibility of change within academia was set forth by Fleming (1990) when she said that there are two keys: 1) curriculum change and 2) enlightened faculty and staff. However, securing financial resources for diversity is an easier task than securing enlightened and committed people, especially those who will make the significant changes via personal transformation and curriculum changes.

In ancient times Plato said, "A society cultivates whatever is honored there." At the University of Louisville we have taken steps to honor diversity with a university-wide celebration and we know our work is not done.

During the week-long celebration there were moments of silence and others of controversy. Students, faculty, staff, alumni, and the community shared heartfelt concerns with disarming candor. Speaker presentations were designed to challenge, to engender commitments, and to help cure the insidious evils of cultural and racial prejudice. Achieving, respecting, accepting, and embracing diversity is a complex and demanding mission. It goes to the core essence of everyone's mind and heart. At the University of Louisville there is a willingness to go further because, in the words of Roger Douglas, the chair of the Pan African Studies Department, "The planners of the Celebration of Diversity at the University of Louisville can consider themselves part of a select few in the United States who are attempting to recall and reshape the ethical and moral consciousness of our nation."

September 8-18, 1990, is now history, and a good history. The future is now before us and when that too becomes history, our deepest and abiding hope is that it will be a much better history than the one we inherited.

References

"A Bowlful of Opportunity." (1990, December 30). *The Courier Journal*, p. D2.

Carnegie Foundation for the Advancement of Teaching, The. (1990). *Campus life: In search of community*. Princeton, N.J.: author.

Fleming, J. (1990, September 11). Presentation made at First Annual Celebration of Diversity. University of Louisville.

Green, M.F. (1989). *Minorities on campus: A handbook for enhancing diversity*. Washington, D.C.: American Council on Education.

Ravitch, D. (1990, Summer). Multiculturalism. *American Scholar*, 59(3), 337-354.

Smith, D.G. (1989). *The challenge of diversity: Involvement or alienation in the academy?* ASHE/ERIC Report No. 5. Washington, D.C.: ERIC Clearinghouse on Higher Education.

Washington, V., and Harvey, W. (1989). *Affirmative rhetoric, negative action: African-American and Hispanic faculty at predominantly white institutions*. ASHE/ERIC Report No. 2. Washington, D.C.: ERIC Clearinghouse on Higher Education.

CHAPTER SIX

The Faculty Response to Campus Climate Issues

Shirley Stennis Williams

Astin (1982) and Fleming (1984) have argued that campus climate is one of the most important but most difficult to measure variables in the progress-to-graduation rate of minorities on predominantly white campuses. Fleming (1984) and Egerton (1982) suggested that for this and other reasons, African American students, in particular, should expect greater success in same-race institutions. Yet despite the availability of minority-dominant institutions for Hispanics and Native Americans, and 110 institutions that are historically African American, the majority of minority students still attend college in predominantly white institutions (Allen, Haddad & Kirkland, 1984; American Council on Education and Education Commission of the States 1988; American Council on Education, 1989).

The author is indebted to Hazel Symonette and Mary Hartl Biel for their assistance in the preparation of this paper.

Throughout the 1980s predominantly white institutions have experienced a rising tide of race-related incidents that have disrupted the campus lives of African American, Hispanic, Native American, and Asian ethnic groups and other minority groups such as gays, lesbians, Muslims, and Jews. At Michigan State University, Asian American students were verbally abused on the student radio station and graffiti was sprayed on their dorm doors; at Harvard University, a student hung a Dixie-crested flag from her window; at the University of Wisconsin-Madison, fraternity students donned black faces as part of their "historic" fall celebration, and in a second incident, another fraternity used a wooden statue of a dark-skinned man to promote its annual Fiji Island party (Farrell 1988a, 1988b; McBay, 1986; Perlez, 1987). Campuses across the nation have experienced ethnic conflict and been forced to deal with overt and covert ethnic harassment because of similar incidents (Farrell 1988c, 1988d).

For several reasons that surely include campus and classroom climate, underserved minority groups such as African Americans, Hispanics, and Native Americans have dismal records in postsecondary education. They continue to graduation at rates that are much lower than those of whites; they are underrepresented in most disciplines; and in such critical fields as computer science, advanced degrees are almost nonexistent. The number earning doctorates is declining and the poor college-going rates for African American males are alarming. Even in two-year colleges where African American males are most heavily represented, the rate of continuation of two-year graduates to four-year degrees is disappointing (Adolphus, 1984; American Council on Education, 1989; Greene, 1989; Peer, 1981; University of the State of New York, 1984).

The term *minority* has lost its statistical meaning in many areas of the country, including at least 22 of the 25 largest school districts in the nation, four states, and the District of Columbia. All are now majority minority (Quality Education for Minorities Project, 1990; Hodgkinson, 1985). Youth from these and other diverse communities will comprise a large part of the generation that is expected to fulfill the six ambitious goals of Education 2000, that include a requirement that every child come to school ready to learn, that literacy become a priority, and most notably, the challenge that American youth will outperform those from other nations in math and science by the year 2000 (U.S. Department of Education, 1987, 1991).

While education is continually cited by minority parents as their first priority, it is clear that minorities are losing ground in America's four-year colleges and universities. Although the high school graduation rates of minorities continue to climb, minorities are not receiving college degrees in proportion to their share of the college-age population. Even more alarming is the dropout rate of minority students who were fully admitted to the university. Campus climate is second only to adequate finances as the reason given for nonpersistence in college (Commission for Reviewing the Master Plan for Higher Education, 1987).

THE UNIVERSITY OF WISCONSIN SYSTEM DESIGN FOR DIVERSITY

In 1987 when African Americans, Hispanics, Native Americans, and Asian Americans entered the 13 campuses of the University of Wisconsin System, they found that they were among 7,500 similar students whom the university had

classified as underserved minority groups (University of
Wisconsin System, 1988a). They and their ethnic group peers
were thrust into campuses amid approximately 150,220 other
students, most of whom were white and most of whom were
undergraduates. When these students entered the classroom,
they discovered that there were few minority faculty and
nonfaculty instructional staff. There were 420 African
American, Hispanic, Asian American, and Native American
faculty compared to 66,698 white faculty. There were similar
figures for noninstructional academic staff — 415 to 5,505.
Despite the Board of Regents' ambitious minority recruitment
goals in its required annual reports since the 1970s, few real
gains were noted in the 1980s (University of Wisconsin
System, 1988b, 1989).

In addition, the campus environment at these institutions
was less than hospitable for "other" students. They often
turned to ethnic centers, ethnic residence halls, and other
refuges from the largely all-white world that they had entered
(Williams, Terrell & Haynes, 1988).

Near the end of his first year as president of the University
of Wisconsin System, Kenneth Shaw presented the Board of
Regents with his vision to address the endemic problem of
underrepresentation of minorities in the system (University
of Wisconsin System, 1987). Shaw warned that diversity
must not continue to be the province of a few beleaguered
minority program specialists; it should be a jointly valued
commitment that would be defended by faculty and student
affairs professionals. He, like Wilkerson (1989), challenged
faculty to embrace diversity to better teach all of the
disciplines.

DiBaggio (1989) and El-Khawas (1989) claimed that such
presidential level leadership is crucial in setting a tone for
changes that are highly controversial. During the first two

years of his tenure, Shaw pushed forward over 100 policy initiatives, including at least ten that were related to minority students and faculty. Many of these were embodied in *Planning the Future* (University of Wisconsin System, 1986), a major policy document that aimed to solidify the merger of the two former state university systems. This document initiated faculty involvement in equity issues with the following recommendations in the equity resolution:

❐ A minority graduate incentive program will be established as a grow-your-own program for minority faculty in the system. The plan will require additional funding in order to focus dollars on underrepresented minority doctoral students who have an interest in college teaching. Incentives will be provided to the University of Wisconsin System graduates who remain within the University of Wisconsin System to teach.

❐ A faculty retention project will be developed that will include a faculty mentor program whereby junior minority faculty members have the option to work with a senior faculty member. On a carefully selected basis, pretenure Hispanic, African American, and Native American faculty will be provided released time and stipends to develop and complete research projects.

❐ A University of Wisconsin System-wide Institute for Race and Ethnic Studies will be created at one of the University of Wisconsin institutions. The institute will include positions for research faculty.

❐ Each institution will establish a faculty and staff committee on affirmative action for minority faculty and staff. The committee will address issues of recruiting, evaluation and promotion and seek innovative and creative methods of improving the institution's record of employing and retaining underrepresented minorities.

❏ The president will convene a conference of underrepresented minority faculty. This group shall make recommendations to the president on minority student and faculty needs.

❏ The president will appoint a system-wide study group on the status of minority faculty and staff to advise him on ways to improve the position of minorities in the University of Wisconsin System (p. A22).

On April 7, 1988, the Board of Regents adopted the far-reaching University of Wisconsin System (1988a) Design for Diversity. The program was intended to be a comprehensive plan to increase diversity on all campuses within the University of Wisconsin System. The plan embraced reports from a variety of groups, task forces, and committees that had been appointed under the equity component of Planning the Future, and other resources. There were seven major goals:

Goal One: Recognize the need to eliminate the underrepresentation of minority and economically disadvantaged people in the University of Wisconsin System.

Goal Two: Educate all students for an increasingly multicultural society in Wisconsin, our nation and the world.

Goal Three: Improve recruiting and retention efforts to better enable targeted minority students* to enroll more easily and function more effectively at our universities.

---

*Minority students means students who are African American, Hispanic, Native American, or certain Asian minorities (Asians who have been admitted to the United States after December 31, 1975, and who either are former citizens of Laos, Vietnam, or Cambodia or whose ancestors were or are citizens of Laos, Vietnam, or Cambodia).

Goal Four: Improve evaluation efforts in the areas of minority student enrollment/retention and faculty/staff recruitment and retention.

Goal Five: Remove financial barriers that prevent minorities and economically disadvantaged people from viewing college as a realistic option.

Goal Six: Increase the number of minority faculty and staff throughout the University of Wisconsin System.

Goal Seven: Establish effective partnerships with the public schools, the Vocational, Technical and Adult Education (VTAE) System, state government, the community and the private sector to assist the University of Wisconsin System's efforts to improve minority education.

To address these goals, the design recommended programs to enhance: (1) student access and retention, (2) the multicultural environment in the classroom and around the campus, (3) financial aid services, (4) the system's cooperative efforts with the Department of Public Instruction (K-12) and the VTAE System, and (5) system administration organization.

There were two emphases that addressed academic climate. One required a campus-level academic program that would broaden the general education requirements to include ethnic studies (University of Wisconsin System, 1988a):

> Each institution must show that it has organized instruction or
> programs on race and ethnicity as part of every student's
> undergraduate educational experience; and [is] integrating ethnic
> studies into existing courses (p. 3).

In 1989, a system-wide conference to foster the implementation of this requirement was held under the theme, "The Challenge of Diversity: Curriculum Development for the 21st Century." Other curriculum development conferences were sponsored by the Institute on Race and Ethnicity.

The second academic emphasis addressed the need of each student to study and live in an environment that was free of any form of ethnic harassment (University of Wisconsin System, 1988a):

> Each institution will develop codes of student and employee
> conduct to ensure a nondiscriminatory environment. System
> guidelines will be prepared for institutional use by July 1, 1988.
> Codes should deal with both individuals and student organizations
> that might be charged with discriminatory activity and other forms
> of racism and harassment. These codes shall be in effect no later
> than January 1989 (p. 3).

This requirement, commonly referred to as "the UWS-17," (Chapter 17.06) received wide attention from the media because of concern that it infringed on First Amendment rights. Some faculty were concerned that classroom discussion could be affected. Yet notable faculty law scholars assured the administration that Chapter UWS-17.06 was defensible and could stand as written.

Many controversial initiatives flounder when there are no resources. Accordingly, as part of this effort, two funds of up to $100,000 were designated to match and encourage institutional efforts to improve the ethnic studies curricula and special programs in the University of Wisconsin System and to provide faculty and academic staff development funds for programs to improve the multicultural environment or address issues of race and ethnicity. Two of the most promising resource rewards were (1) the creation of 49 new faculty lines to increase faculty diversity and (2) the creation of a minority stars fund (a subset of an existing stars fund) that was designed to retain or hire minority faculty with national reputations by matching offers from competing universities (University of Wisconsin System, 1986, 1988b, 1989).

An important part of the Design for Diversity required each chancellor to coordinate the development of the institutional plan, and to ensure that the plan included faculty, staff, students and administration. The chancellors of the two doctoral campuses developed complete institutional plans that often exceeded the requirements of the Design for Diversity. In addition, the system president publicly affirmed that the institution's success in meeting these requirements would be a significant part of each chancellor's annual evaluation (University of Wisconsin System, 1988a).

In a major address to a conference on minority demographics and higher education, Shaw (1988) discussed some major conditions that must be met if institutions were to be agents of change for diversity:

> 1. People in organizations not only listen to what their leaders say; they watch closely what is done. If there are no people of color . . . if there are no women . . . on the president's or chancellor's executive team, no amount of rhetoric will obscure this deficiency.
>
> 2. While it is important to refer to national conditions, the main thrust of institutional [commitment] must address the local situation.
>
> 3. Without specific goals there are no benchmarks against which success can be measured.

4.Targets for recruitment and retention of faculty and students should force the institution to stretch and to make significant improvements. These goals should require sustained commitment from the entire staff and student body.

5.If the goals are important [the institution] must plan appropriate rewards and punishments to encourage their achievement.

6.[The institution] must provide the [resources] that will help the willing. . .become the able (pp. 3-4).

THE STUDY

There are several assumptions and consequences of the sections on academic reform within the Design for Diversity. While one intent was to ensure that the University of Wisconsin System faculty become equal partners with noninstructional staff in addressing one of the most serious problems facing universities, the academic reforms in fact had mixed results from the viewpoint of minority student affairs professionals.

To assess how student affairs professionals viewed the academic reform section, the author conducted a telephone survey of senior minority program staff at each of the 13 four-year campuses of the University of Wisconsin System. The interview questionnaire included 10 close-ended items, each with three response categories: "Generally effective," "No effect" and " Generally ineffective." Responses to each question were examined for comments and elaboration.

Thirteen professionals participated in the interviews. Each was the senior professional in minority affairs at his/her institution. The University of Wisconsin System requires each institution name a minority-disadvantaged program administrator. Four were women and nine were men. The ethnic mix was seven African American, two Hispanic, three Native American, and one Asian American. In addition to their administrative titles, two were also tenured faculty, one was untenured faculty, and the remainder were untenured administrators (ranging from the director to the assistant vice chancellor levels). The years of service of the faculty and minority program administrators at the assistant vice chancellor level ranged from 5 to 23 with a mean of 16 years. The years of service of the other minority program respondents ranged from 2 to 18 with a mean of slightly over 5 years.

The writer cautions the reader that the data presented here have limitations. The survey was limited to only those initiatives to improve campus climate that involve faculty. Initiatives that involve nonfaculty professionals alone were not within the scope of the study. Also, a decision was made to survey only senior minority program professionals. Although this report includes that total population, the aggregate number of respondents was limited. Finally, because of the small number of respondents and the need to maintain confidentiality, it was not possible to fully describe the ethnic variability in response patterns. Despite these limits, the writer is confident that the study will be of interest to campuses that are also considering greater collaboration among faculty and minority student services professionals to address intractable campus climate issues and concerns.

The Survey

The survey that was used in the study consisted of ten questions. Six questions were related to the University of

Wisconsin System's goals to develop a faculty cohort that was ethnically diverse. New faculty programs that were designed to create a campus climate that would foster diversity among faculty were described and respondents rated them. Activities that were presented included system-wide minority faculty conferences, senior mentors for minority faculty, research buy-outs for minority faculty, the grow-your-own-professor program for minority doctoral students, a study group to advise the university system president on minority faculty activities, and the affirmative action committee.

Four questions were related to curriculum activities from the Design for Diversity Program. Respondents were asked to rate the effectiveness of each activity for improving campus climate. One of the activities to be rated was the set-aside of $100,000 to develop projects to improve the ethnic studies curricula. Faculty could apply for small research grants to improve their courses or workshops that were related to diversity. A second fund that provided funds for joint faculty and nonfaculty programs to address issues of race and ethnicity was also rated.

The Findings
The findings indicated that while minority professionals seek the involvement of faculty in efforts to improve campus climate for faculty and students from all ethnic backgrounds, the minority affairs professionals are unsure of how effective such involvement is on the predominantly white campuses in this study. The perceived success or failure of selected efforts are discussed below.

Senior Faculty Mentors

The climate in the classroom is essential to the academic success of minority students; it is important that they see minority professionals in the careers they hope to enter. Departments should also recognize that all students benefit from having both genders and multiple cultures be a part of their preparation programs. It is clear from the data that designating a senior faculty mentor for junior minority faculty should be practiced by most institutions. Respondents thought this had been one of the most effective initiatives. There were several cautions and caveats about this important initiative. One respondent said,

> The faculty mentor program provides a forum for asking for help and for giving help, but some faculty don't know how to ask for help and some don't know how to give it.

Other respondents offered these comments and suggestions:

> This is very important. But success depends on the resources that the senior member has to share—research skills, department politics know-how, funding sources and especially publication outlets.

> There is not enough thought given to the enormous dissonance that could exist. While mentors of minorities approved this theoretically, mentors need training, particularly on campuses where senior faculty have had no interaction or experience with minorities.

> Ideally, the mentors should be of the same race as the mentee. Then you'd really have help in cutting through . . . Lacking this,

perhaps a second [junior] mentor for social survival could be
named.

The consensus of opinion was that senior faculty mentors
could help the minority professionals immeasurably in the
long march toward tenure. Some felt that there should be
special training for mentors that is comparable to that for
department chairs. A few also felt that the mentor should be
monitored and that if it is apparent that there is not a good
"fit," a change should be made.

Minority Faculty and Staff Conference
Since the Design for Diversity was implemented, there have
been two biennial conferences for minority faculty. Both
conferences were hosted by the University of Wisconsin
System   administration   at   the   University   of
Wisconsin-Madison campus. Responses to the question on
the biennial conference for underrepresented minority faculty
showed the greatest ambivalence. The conference was at first
viewed suspiciously by some nonminority faculty who were
convinced that certain "firebrand" minority faculty would
foment revolution among the "good" ones. Others had to be
assured that the one-day conference was open to all who might
like to attend the lectures or small group sessions.
Respondents doubted whether any substantive changes had
occurred because of the conferences, yet they felt the chance
to interact with the minority body politic or the minority
professoriate was a balm for the spirits for those from outlying
campuses. The following comments reflect the varying
sentiments:

I can't quantify the effectiveness, but meeting other colleagues and being able to share experiences is very useful psychologically. Concrete problems are not resolved, but meeting to network is important. I've found that having a chance to develop minority contacts is very useful.

After the experience, you go back to the same isolation and wait another two years to meet again. Little has changed.

It's great to talk about minority (faculty and staff) concerns, particularly for those isolated on small campuses in small cities.

The first conference was structured for faculty, but both the faculty and staff agreed that, given their small numbers, it was good for later conferences to allow faculty and staff to meet together and develop commonality of purpose and activities. Several suggested that bonds were developed between the minority faculty and the minority staff.

Many respondents felt that campus administrators should attend to hear the minority professionals discuss their concerns. Several suggested that having a select few administrators attend as program presenters was not enough:

The conference provides a release of tension and opportunities for networking. But what is to be attained is not clear. Senior administrators should be there to hear the concerns.

The conference is preaching to the converted. Administrators need to hear this.

There was one suggestion that the conference not be held. Expectation was apparently so high that disappointment was inevitable.

Release Faculty for Research

In doctoral institutions, it is common practice for faculty to set aside 25-100 percent of their time for a research project. The policy under which this is permitted was used to provide similar time for minority professors in the design. However, minority faculty who are also senior minority program professionals, questioned the assumptions that led to the creation of buy-out positions for minority faculty research. One of these assumptions was that junior minority faculty who were making the sometimes difficult adjustment to a small university milieu would have the time to launch personal research while also establishing themselves as teachers. This is particularly problematic for those who are called upon for extensive community and university service to foster minority access and success. Among the comments were these:

> Minority faculty are often heavily involved in outreach and community service which are not recognized [for promotion and tenure] and have limited time to do research.

> On paper this is great. In reality, minority faculty seldom have time to do the paperwork to ever get the grant. They are caught up in services to students and handling their new classes. This won't work on small campuses.

Other respondents saw great possibilities for the program. The locus in the system-wide Institute on Race and Ethnic Studies that is housed on the University of Wisconsin-Milwaukee campus was seen as a more favorable climate for research by minority researchers, although it needs more publicity. This system-wide program also had some strong supporters.

The double jeopardy of minority faculty that has been cited in several studies is quite evident on the campuses of the University of Wisconsin System. Their obligation to "give back" or provide service to their campus and community, while meeting the expectation for tenure and promotion in a sometimes hostile or indifferent environment, creates a double bind that few are able to escape. Several respondents lashed out at the unfairness of a system that gave little credit to minority faculty involvement with minority students, or that would not give more time on the tenure clock when the demands and expectations for a department's minority faculty member became a deterrent to the usual research.

Grow-Your-Own Doctoral Program
The University of Wisconsin hoped to address the continual shortage of minority candidates for faculty positions through an ambitious program of financial incentives to minority postmasters degree students. When nominated for doctoral study by the four-year campuses in the University of Wisconsin System from which they had earned their first graduate degree, students could be supported for study for up to three years. There were mixed views on the University of Wisconsin System's grow-your-own program for minority doctoral students who wanted to teach in one of the four-year institutions. Some thought the $15,000 stipend was too low given the heavy family responsibilities of minority students. They also disapproved of the requirement for full-time study, and for a limitation to study only at the two public doctoral institutions. Some knew of colleagues who had asked that the

existing undergraduate reciprocity with the University of Minnesota be extended to this program.

> There is not enough money in the pot. The tuition reimbursement program is better and you get to keep your job. The amount should be $20-25,000. If you're good, another state will give you more than $15,000.

> We hired one of the people from this program. We support it.

> There is opposition to hiring their own [new] graduates on doctoral campuses. Yet minorities often prefer not to go to small white campuses for their first experience. They won't stay. This program might work better for Wisconsin Native Americans who often live in northern rural areas.

Respondents were somewhat resentful of the grow-your-own program requirement that program participants must accept an offer to teach in the University of Wisconsin System or repay the stipend. One respondent said that the new minority Ph.D. might not prefer to have the first college position be in an uncomfortable environment and one where minority students and their parents would constantly seek them out for assistance with their needs.

One respondent felt that the onerous payback provisions for those who did not accept positions in the University of Wisconsin System might be a problem, and that the system should not feel betrayed if a student accepted a better offer in another state. " It is not a failure if they [graduates] leave. It should be considered a compliment if someone outbids us."

Faculty/Staff Affirmative Action Committees

There were strong feelings that campus affirmative action committees were "rubber stamps" for the affirmative action office, and thus ineffective. The most strongly held position was that affirmative action committees were not proactive in increasing the number of faculty of color. A few respondents openly stated their belief that the committees were strongly slanted toward gender access for nonminorities:

> Affirmative action is too geared toward women, and minority women are ignored.

> I don't know too much about it or the mechanism. Greater commitment is needed and some dollars to get departments to set or meet hiring goals. They [committees] don't have power of the purse strings.

> The challenge is to have administrative support, while remembering that faculty do the hiring in departments. They [faculty] need to be convinced.
> Our committee is basically a rubber stamp. They meet once per semester. I have tried to get on it and can't.

> The affirmative action committee has long been a lightning rod for nonminorities. As the committees have become institutionalized, they are now criticized by both sides. Even ensuring that faculty are on the committees has not yet changed the image of the committees.

Study Group to Advise the President
On the Status of Minority Faculty and Staff

Some people did not remember the work of the system-wide study group on the status of minority faculty and staff. Soon after the report was filed, the principal author left the University of Wisconsin System. However, some respondents said that if the committee report had indeed influenced the president, they approved of the advice that he evidently received. Some said that because they strongly supported the Design for Diversity and some of his other programs and pronouncements, they felt that this was probably an effective initiative. It received an approval rating of greater than 60 percent.

Special Funds to Support Race and Ethnicity Projects
The Design for Diversity included at least four new initiatives related to ethnic studies and to faculty efforts to address ethnicity in the classroom. Beginning in 1989, the University of Wisconsin System created two funds of $100,000 each for program activities in this area. The first fund required an institutional model for campus curriculum projects to address issues of race and ethnicity. The second fund was for faculty and staff development projects to address issues of race and ethnicity and to improve the multicultural environment.

Respondents had some difficulty in separating the two funds and in distinguishing them from other programs related to ethnic programming. Some people felt that the funds were insufficient for 13 campuses, and that the call for proposals was not widely disseminated. Institutional efforts to improve the ethnic studies curricula received an approval rating of greater than 60 percent. Funds for faculty and staff development was viewed much less favorably. Some respondents seemed to feel that doctoral campus researchers would be granted most of the faculty and staff development funds for esoteric research that would do little to improve the knowledge base on the small campuses or inform campus practices. Among the comments were these:

> Our campus did not try for the funds.

> This has not gone far on our campus: the publicity has not been effective.

> Some people here are really pushing ethnic studies.

> Some of the most positive respondents mentioned their use of these funds to bring faculty from historically Black colleges to campus for guest lectureships or faculty exchanges.

Ethnic Course Infusion and Ethnic Graduation Requirement

Two requirements were for curricular changes to (1) integrate ethnic studies into existing courses via an infusion model and (2) require organized instruction or programs as part of every undergraduate's general education, most often via a specific course requirement. More than 84 percent (84.6) of the respondents believed the requirement that faculty infuse ethnicity into their courses was very effective. No respondent labeled this ineffective on the local campus.

Gender

A few tendencies are worthy of note. Female respondents were largely supportive of affirmative action; only one said that it was generally ineffective and biased toward white women. Male respondents, on the other hand, were divided, but largely disapproved of the actions of the faculty/staff committee and believed that the committee was controlled by the administration.

Female respondents also felt that the biennial conference was generally ineffective. It was difficult to tell from their comments, why the female respondents did not value the networking that was mentioned by most male respondents, including those who devalued the conference generally. It might be that the list of speakers was dominated by men, or that there were no structured opportunities for women to talk to each other. At many national conferences, caucuses for women provide opportunities for feminine bonding; perhaps this is needed even more by women in a group that is predominantly minority.

There was no consensus among the women on the faculty time set aside for research. The single positive response came from a respondent who had received one of the grants. Other women were concerned about the competing demands on the minority faculty member's time, or about the fairness of the process for designating the recipients.

Unlike the male respondents, who questioned the level of financial support of the grow-your-own doctoral program, female respondents generally supported the program. Perhaps the $15,000 stipend is not too far removed from the typical pay for 'female' jobs.

Women seemed to value the requirement for full-time study, with one suggesting that this would provide relief from balancing multiple expectations. Female opinions might also have been swayed by the fact that the first two graduates of the program were female, and each accepted an attractive offer that included a tenure line.

Ethnicity

The minorities in the smallest communities often felt isolated from their culture. Such typical and taken-for-granted cultural support as hair stylists, barbers, churches, social groups, public service groups, radio stations, and newspapers are often unavailable in Wisconsin cities of less than 25,000 people. Most important, the respondents alluded to the psychological pressure of always being "in role" as "a minority professional from the college" throughout the community. African Americans were most likely to experience this kind of social distancing.

Because of the small size of the sample, the other ethnic group responses were grouped. Their major concerns centered around developing an on-campus sense of community in the department or administrative unit. As mentioned earlier, one respondent, though not Native American, suggested rural settings might not be as problematic for Wisconsin Native Americans who have more than 10 state tribal groups in different rural areas, in addition to their communities in Milwaukee and Green Bay.

Size of City

The University of Wisconsin System includes campuses in communities and cities of a range of sizes: from rural villages to one of the nation's top cities. The two doctoral campuses are located in the state's largest city and the capital city. However, the cities that rank third and fourth in size have universities that rank in the bottom quartile in size. Were there survey items that were affected by city size? The survey item that yielded the greatest variation among responses based on community size was the requirement for senior faculty mentors. Several responses suggested that the mentor needed to be proactive. There were several allusions to the need for the mentor to assist with activities other than the academic. A few suggested that help from the mentor to fit into the community would be desirable.

Size of community also seemed to be a variable in the respondent's assessment of the nontenure-related expectations that minority students and student affairs professionals hold for minority faculty. In larger communities, both students and faculty can escape the predominantly white campus and establish alliances, networks and support groups in the surrounding community. In the small town, there is no escape and there is a strong expectation that the minority faculty will assist the 18-year-old minority freshman to achieve a "comfort level" in the new home. There was little recognition that the minority faculty member was thus responsible for the social well-being of him/herself and his/her family and the students. Often the student's family would specifically ask the faculty member from their cultural group to "Please look out for Johnny while he's here." Minority faculty felt that the mentor training should include helping the new minority faculty member to assist these disparate groups to feel at home and develop a feeling of community in the small town environment.

Size of community was also a likely variable in concerns expressed about the grow-your-own program. There was some resistance by northern university staff to traveling to the southern urbanized end of the state to pursue doctoral study. One small town respondent complained that students should be allowed to attend northern doctoral campuses, even though these are in Minnesota.

Size of University
For this study, universities have been categorized by size into three groups. The doctoral campuses have more than 20,000 students, small universities have fewer than 5,000 and mid size universities include those between 5,000-20,000. Faculty in smaller and medium sized institutions often have proportionately heavier teaching loads. In small universities, all of the faculty teach graduate and undergraduate classes and advise students. There are few graduate or teaching assistants. The students come from a limited geographical base and expect personalized attention. Respondents questioned whether such programs as releasing faculty for research are realistic for these small campuses. When everyone in the department has heavy advising, teaching, and committee responsibilities, and when the community lacks a cadre of highly educated adjunct faculty, seeking such a reward might be considered disloyal, since typically, other department members would have to cover the recipient's released time.

Size of a university was also considered important in the mentor's initiative since a small university faculty member might have fewer career perks than those on larger campuses, e.g., named chairs, large extramural grants, and publishing contracts. Thus, small campus senior faculty might have little to offer the junior faculty member that would be career advancing, other than "old boy network" congeniality.

SUMMARY AND RECOMMENDATIONS

The University of Wisconsin System recognized that demographic changes were transforming the student pool for its predominantly white universities — making it increasingly multi-ethnic. Yet African American, Hispanic, Native American, and Southeast Asian students — its historically underserved minorities — were facing increasing racial and ethnic harassment and "chilly" classrooms in its far-flung campuses. In addition, despite annual reports on minority access, the numbers were stagnant. Accordingly, the system established conditions and goals that should be met in its ambitious reform-for-diversification program. These conditions and goals included curricula changes and programs to increase the number of minority faculty and improve their potential for tenure. Lastly, the chancellor of each institution was to be the recognized leader of the initiatives to improve the academic climate for minority students and faculty. Each institution developed its own strategies for meeting the system-wide goals. In addition, the doctoral institutions developed major corollary plans for diversity.

This study has examined the effectiveness to date of faculty activities that were required or recommended under the Design for Diversity and its predecessor, Planning for the Future. The initiatives were viewed through the prism of minority student affairs professionals, who often serve as an important link between student services and academic programs.

From the perspective of senior minority professionals, the following recommendations should be implemented on any campus that plans to improve the academic climate for diversity:

> ❐ Senior faculty mentors for minority junior faculty should be encouraged. An orientation should be provided for mentors and periodic assessments should be made of the continuing "fit."

❒ An ethnic studies requirement should be initiated by the faculty, with strong support by the administration. The requirement should be similar to the non-Western or other general education course requirement. Majority and minority student support should be sought.

❒ Ethnic studies should be integrated into existing courses. Funds and other incentives should be provided to assist faculty in diversification of the curriculum.

❒ The president and other senior administrators should be actively involved in campus efforts to enhance the academic climate for diversity.

❒ The special services rendered to students, other faculty and staff and the community by minority faculty on a predominantly white campus should be recognized for promotion, tenure and merit.

❒ The president and other senior administrators should recognize that opportunities to network among minority faculty in similar institutions are essential for job satisfaction, career development [advancement] and, thus, retention.

❒ Faculty/staff affirmative action committees should be operated like other all-campus committees. They should not be tied to an administrative office, namely, the affirmative action office. The committees should be equally sensitive to ethnic, gender and other campus bias issues.

❒ Research opportunities should be structured with minority input to ensure that they address the needs and interests of minority faculty.

References

Adolphus, S. (Ed.). (1984). *Equality postponed: Continuing barriers to higher education in the 1980s.* Report from a policy conference on postsecondary programs for the disadvantaged. New York: College Entrance Examination Board.

Allen, W.R., Haddad, A., and Kirkland, M. (1984, November). *Preliminary report: 1982 graduate professional survey, national study of black college students.* Ann Arbor, Michigan: University of Michigan Center for Afro-American Studies.

American Council on Education (1989). *Minorities in higher education.* Washington, D.C.: author.

American Council on Education and Education Commission of the States (1988). *One-third of a nation: A report of the commission on minority participating in education and American life.* Washington, D.C.: author.

Astin, A. (1982). *Minorities in American higher education.* San Francisco: Jossey-Bass.

Commission for Reviewing the Master Plan for Higher Education (1987). *The master plan reviewed: Unity, equity, quality and efficiency in California postsecondary education.* Sacramento, California: author.

DiBaggio, J.A. (1989). The president's role in the quality of campus life. *Educational Record,* 70(3/4), 8-12.

Egerton, J. (1982). *Race and equity in higher education.* Washington, D.C.: American Council on Education.

El-Khawas, E. (1989). Ways to improve campus life: What the president suggests. *Educational Record*, X(X), 10-11.

Farrell C.S. (1988a, January 27). Black students seen facing "new racism" on many campuses. *The Chronicle of Higher Education,* pp. A1, A37-38.

Farrell, C.S. (1988b, January 27). Stung by racial incidents and charges of indifference, Berkeley to become model integrated university. *The Chronicle of Higher Education*, pp. A37-38.

Farrell, C.S. (1988c, February 17). Rising concerns over campus racial bias marked at Northern Illinois University. *The Chronicle of Higher Education*, p. A37-38.

Farrell, C.S. (1988d, February 24). Students protesting racial bias at University of Massachusetts end occupation of campus building after 5 days. *The Chronicle of Higher Education*, p. A41.

Fleming, J. (1984). *Blacks in college.* San Francisco: Jossey-Bass.

Greene, M.T. (Ed.).(1989). *Minorities on campus: A handbook for enhancing diversity.* Washington, D.C.: American Council on Education.

Hodgkinson, H.L. (1985). *All one system: Demographics of education — Kindergarten through graduate school.* (The Educational Resources Information Center, Document #ED 261101). Washington, D.C.: Institute for Educational Leadership.

McBay, S.M. (1986). *The racial climate on the MIT campus: A report of the minority student issues group.* Cambridge:

Massachusetts Institute of Technology, Office of the Dean of Student Affairs.

Peer, J.L. (1981). *Minority access to higher education.* AAHE-ERIC/Higher Education Research Report No. 1. Washington, D.C.: ERIC Clearinghouse on Higher Education.

Perlez, J. (1987). Campus race incidents disquiet University of Michigan. *New York Times,* p. 8.

Quality Education for Minorities Project (1990). *Education that works: An action plan for the education of minorities.* Cambridge, Massachusetts: Massachusetts Institute of Technology.

Shaw, K.A. (1988, July). Taking charge. A presentation to the conference, Educating One-Third of a Nation, Washington, D.C.

U.S. Department of Education (1987). *Trends in minority enrollment in higher education.* Washington, D.C.: author.

U.S. Department of Education (1991). *America 2000: An education strategy sourcebook.* Washington, D.C.: author.

University of the State of New York, The (1984). Increasing minority access to the licensed professions: A regent action paper. Albany, New York: State Education Department.

University of Wisconsin System (1986). *Planning the future: Report of the regents on the future of the University of Wisconsin System.* Madison, Wisconsin: Board of Regents.

University of Wisconsin System (1987). *Annual report to the Regents on 1985-86 progress and achievement of goals for*

American racial and ethnic minority students. Madison, Wisconsin: Board of Regents.

University of Wisconsin System (1988a, April). Design for diversity: A report to the Board of Regents by president Kenneth A. Shaw. Unpublished.

University of Wisconsin System (1988b). Annual report to the Board of Regents on 1986-87 progress and achievement of goals for American racial and ethnic minority students. Unpublished.

University of Wisconsin System (1989). Annual report to the Board of Regents on 1987-88 progress and achievement of goals for American racial and ethnic minority students. Unpublished.

Wilkerson, M. (1989). *The curriculum and cultural diversity.* New York: The College Board, Office of Academic Affairs.

Williams, S.S., Terrell, M., and Haynes, A. (1988). The emergent role of multicultural education centers on predominantly white campuses. In M. Terrell and D. Wright (Eds.), *From survival to success: Promoting minority student retention* (pp. 73-98). Washington, D.C.: National Association of Student Personnel Administrators.

CHAPTER SEVEN

Perceptions and Views of Racism
A Student Leader's Perspective

Bruce D. La Vant
Charles L. Brown
Emmanuel Newsome

As discussed in previous chapters, the problem of racism continues to be a prevalent issue on college and university campuses throughout the country. Many institutions of higher learning have been plagued with problems such as racist assaults and overt discrimination. Magner (1990) stated that many examples could be cited of "ugly racist incidents," which appear to be, for the most part, incidents that involve black and white students. Ignorance, lack of understanding, and general disrespect for others are characteristics of college students which lead to racism on campus.

College presidents, vice presidents of student affairs, and other college administrators have received numerous incident reports of racial harassment of students: the initials "KKK" carved in an African American student's room, a caricature affixed to a Black Student Association bulletin board of an African American overlaid with the international symbol for the forbidden, Asian students told by white students to leave a residence hall, racial jokes broadcast over a university radio station, and racist letters sent to Hispanic students in a campus residence hall (Rodriques, 1989).

Such incidents impede institutional efforts to promote an appreciation of cultural and ethnic diversity on campus by enhancing and increasing minority student access, retention, and graduation. Students, faculty, administrators, and community leaders at such institutions have engaged in renewed efforts to combat these problems and issues. Many preventive strategies have been introduced on campuses throughout the nation in an attempt to create environments more inviting for all racial and ethnic groups.

Many of these efforts have been organized and promoted by student leaders. Generally, these efforts have taken on the form of antiracism training (Carter, 1990). The views and perceptions that students leaders have developed concerning racism, racist attitudes, and, more specifically, a lack of morals and values that threaten racial harmony merit attention.

STUDENT LEADERS AS
VALUABLE RESOURCES

Because of a resurgence in the commitment to create and maintain culturally diverse and pluralistic college campuses, students of all racial and ethnic backgrounds are often consulted regarding issues that will affect entire campus communities. Such students often assume roles, responsibilities, and leadership positions that many student affairs professionals rely upon to develop and provide quality services to their universities.

On many campuses — large and small, public and private — faculty and staff have their own ideas and perceptions about how racism is affecting their campus environment. Oftentimes, many appear to be ignorant of the issue of racism and deny that it exists on their particular campuses. Student leaders and aspiring student leaders, however, are often more aware of the critical issues affecting their campuses. Thus, student leaders are vital resources who can provide valid recommendations, comments, and strategies to assist in ridding a campus of racism.

To this end, it is valuable to explore further the possibilities of relying upon student leaders as resource persons on racism. It is, therefore, important to examine the race-related problems that student leaders encounter as they attempt to improve their campus environments.

STUDENT LEADERSHIP STYLES, PERCEPTIONS, AND RACISM

Some educators believe that ethnic minority and white students differ in their perception of multicultural awareness and racism. The difference tends to be greater between African American and Caucasian students. This difference usually affects the leadership styles of both African American and white students who aspire to campus leadership positions.

Minority students, African American students in particular, are more likely to describe their college racial climate as analogous to that of the larger society. On the other hand, white students, by and large, believe racism is not prevalent, and that their campus climate is basically warm, friendly, and inviting to all students. This prevailing belief continues to exist even though many ethnic minority students report that they do not feel welcome on campus and oftentimes are treated like uninvited guests (Parker & Scott, 1985).

Many white students believe minority students' feelings of isolation and exclusion are self-imposed. These students believe that minority students do not try hard enough to become full participants in the campus community. They point to segregated tables in dining halls, segregated intramural athletic teams, requests for separate housing accommodations, and segregated patterns of social interaction on campus (Bloom, 1987).

Troy Duster (cited in Magner, 1990), a professor of sociology and director of the Institute for the Study of Social Change, stated that on predominantly white campuses, it is common for African American, Chicano, or other minority students to feel comfortable by banding together. On the other hand, white students on those campuses don't feel embattled.

Several studies indicate that many minority students experience a greater range of problems in their efforts to adjust socially, psychologically, and academically to the university environment (Gibbs, 1975). In a survey conducted by the Southern Regional Education Board, 40 percent of all African American students attending predominantly white colleges said that they would not select the same college again, but only 20 percent of the white students indicated this feeling (Gibbs, 1975).

African Americans perceive a high degree of discrimination reflected in the campus climate and in the attitudes and behavior of white faculty and students toward them as individuals. Livingston and Stewart's (1987) study of minority students on a large predominantly white university campus found that over 60 percent of those responding indicated that they would not have problems living with a white roommate, 77 percent indicated that they would not have a problem mixing socially with white students. However, 54 percent of these same students expressed frustration because of personal experiences with discrimination, which they attributed to white students' attitudes toward minority students in general.

In another study comparing African American and white attitudes toward integration on a deep-south campus, white students endorsed significantly more negative stereotypes of their "African-American" peers (Muir, 1990). In this study, African American students were stereotyped as shiftless, lazy, lacking ambition, untrustworthy, and vengeful by their white peers. This study also found that 11 percent of the white students felt that African Americans who attend "white" universities become officious, overbearing and disagreeable; 7 percent felt that African Americans cannot compete intellectually with whites.

Despite efforts to explore new and creative ways to promote cultural diversity and increase interaction among the various citizen groups in the academic community, we still find students seeking out those with whom they can identify and relate. Social psychologists refer to this process as "the consciousness of oneness" or "the consciousness of kind." This selective association develops an awareness of commonality with others which in turn creates an in-group sense of empathy and sympathy with them (Zandem, 1987).

The desire to identify with one's own kind can cause a reluctance to interact in one's social environment. This occurrence is referred to as social distance by sociologists

(Theodorson & Theodorson, 1990). As a result of these factors, students and others who conform to social distance behavior often display their ignorance of others by engaging in acts of racial violence.

Many campus leaders associate with persons who have similar interests and thus have very little understanding of issues and concerns of those outside their social circle. This pattern of ethnocentric separatism can be devastating for student leadership on campus. Such student leaders cannot formulate inclusive campus organizational policies nor can they understand the needs of peers who are not a part of their social groups. However, other student leaders have exhibited their sensitivity to and knowledge of other cultural and racial groups.

In a study involving African American and white students, Giobetti, Giobetti, Brown, and Smith (1991) found that 59.8 percent of the African American students who responded had been taught by members of another race, compared to 38.4 percent of white respondents. Five percent of the white students had never had a teacher of another race or ethnic background as compared to 1.1 percent of the African American students. This study also revealed that increased interaction between white and African American students created a higher degree of awareness and concern about minority student issues on campuses. It also indicated that extreme differences in perception of racism among student leaders might be reduced if minority and majority students interacted and socialized more freely on campus.

These studies illustrate clear differences of opinion between minority and majority students about campus life and perceptions of racism. They also highlight a dual cultural system which influences leadership styles. Students who lack contact and interaction with persons of different ethnic groups and socioeconomic backgrounds do not have inclusive leadership philosophies. They are more likely to be insensitive and insecure with people who are different, and their leadership style reflects this feeling. Their opinions on racial and cultural issues probably differ greatly from those of their peers who are different socially and especially ethnically. However, as noted earlier, in examining the existence of racism on college and university campuses, their opinions are of value.

Methodology

To confirm further student leaders' perceptions of racism, the authors employed a stratified random sampling procedure and evaluated student leaders' perceptions on three major university campuses in three different states. The University of Alabama and the University of Toledo are two major research institutions with student populations of more than 20,000. Florida Atlantic University is a large, four-year public institution which enrolls over 10,000 students.

Because of the paucity of empirical research examining perceptions of racism on college and university campuses, the survey instrument used for data collection in this study was reproduced from a document entitled "Combatting Campus Racism" developed by the University of Cincinnati in 1987. This survey was distributed to students at the University of Cincinnati to assess their attitudes toward racism on their campus.

When comparing the present study to the University of Cincinnati's study, one should note that several differences existed with respect to the format and administration of the survey. In the Cincinnati study, a randomly selected sample of full- and part-time students on campus were telephoned and asked to respond to 14 short questions on a five-point scale, ranging from "Strongly Agree" to "Strongly Disagree." The sample consisted of 142 students: 122 white, 11 African American, and 9 representing other minority groups.

By contrast, the sample surveyed in this study consisted of students who served as elected leaders. The survey instrument was distributed to each student leader, and the researchers collected it in approximately 20-30 minutes (see Appendix B). Of the 200 questionnaires distributed, 179 were judged valid for evaluation and analysis. The population that completed valid questionnaires included 113 whites, 43 African Americans, 14 Hispanics, and 7 Asians (see Tables 1, 2, and 3). The survey respondents answered most of the questions; those with no responses were noted in the analysis. In addition, some surveys included specific

Table 1
Survey Respondents

	Frequency	Percent	Valid Percent	Cumulative Percent
Florida Atlantic Univ.	103	57.5	57.5	57.5
Univ. of Alabama	40	22.3	22.3	79.9
Univ. of Toledo	36	20.1	20.1	100.0
Total	179	100.0	100.0	

Valid Cases   179   Missing Cases   0

Table 2
Race of Respondents

	Frequency	Percent	Valid Percent	Cumulative Percent
White	113	63.1	63.5	63.5
Black	43	24.0	24.2	24.2
Hispanic	14	7.8	7.9	95.5
Asian	7	3.9	3.9	99.4
Other	1	.6	.6	100.0
Non Response	1	.6		
Total	179	100.0	100.0	

Valid Cases 178   Missing Cases 1

Table 3
Sex of Respondents

	Frequency	Percent	Valid Percent	Cumulative Percent
Male	78	43.6	44.1	44.1
Female	99	55.3	55.9	100.0
Non Response	2	1.1	Missing	
Total	179	100.0	100.0	

questions on racist or controversial events which occurred on a particular campus (i.e., University of Alabama, etc.).

Results
There were several findings in this survey. Student leaders at all three universities tended to agree that racism is a serious issue at the national and campus levels. However, 25 percent of the students surveyed believed that racism was even more

prevalent on their particular campus than on other campuses. In addition, 43.8 percent of the students surveyed felt that racism affected student/faculty relationships. However, 26.7 percent of the students were neutral about the issue.

In terms of social interaction, other interesting patterns emerged. A large percentage of students, specifically 58.2 percent, reported that they approved of interracial friendships. However, 43.2 percent of the respondents did not approve of interracial dating. These responses imply that casual and social friendships are acceptable campus norms, but relationships that involve male/female romance between the races are unacceptable norms.

A lack of meaningful interaction between black and white students may be a problem on these campuses. The student leaders were almost equally split on whether African Americans like white Americans. Approximately 28 percent agreed that African Americans like white Americans, and 28.4 percent disagreed. In contrast, 43.2 percent responded neutral to this item. Most (78.7 percent) agreed that racial prejudice is still very common. Moreover, 35.6 percent indicated that they had made racist comments and jokes among college peers, but over half (53.4 percent) had not experienced or been part of a racist incident. The student leaders in this survey had mixed opinions on the value and effectiveness of affirmative action programs and activities: 22.2 percent agreed that it is an effective way to remedy past racial discrimination, 38 percent disagreed and 39.8 percent were neutral. Lastly, even though student leaders expressed mixed feelings about affirmative action, 75.3 percent indicated that they believe multicultural programs are beneficial and can help eliminate racism.

DISCUSSION

Students who hold leadership positions play a very important role in their institutions' futures. Much of their leadership influences the type of campus environment and nature of the student body. As the studies cited in this chapter indicate, student leaders are in direct contact with many students who are from various cultural and ethnic backgrounds. They are also in social circles with others who are similar to themselves. Student leaders are also in contact with administration, faculty, staff, and community groups. Therefore, we must accept the notion that student leaders are a good resource about racism on campus.

However, we must understand that students will be at various levels of cultural understanding and awareness. Thus, even student leaders' perceptions of racism on their particular campus will vary. This study demonstrates that variance. While some students were parallel in their thinking, others were unsure about their perceptions.

It is incumbent upon student affairs professionals to continue to utilize student leaders as advisors on matters related to race relations. If student affairs professionals include student leaders in program planning designed to address racism and cultural diversity, the possibilities for experiencing immediate positive results are excellent. Student leaders are also capable of developing campus-based, community-wide programs to address the issue of racism. Student leaders also can assist with modifying attitudes and in creating forums to discuss cultural differences.

The replication of this study on college campuses in other areas of the country should be undertaken to investigate this problem further.

RECOMMENDATIONS

❐ Senior student affairs officers should rely upon student leaders as advisors in the development of training programs to improve the campus climate.

❐ Researchers should continue to evaluate and assess race relations on our campuses and provide information to chief executive officers and student leaders.

❐ The socialization patterns of African American students on predominantly white campuses should be explored.

❐ Student leaders should attempt to expose all students to multicultural and multi-ethnic awareness training by actively promoting student involvement.

❐ Student leaders must require all individuals who work on their particular campus to attend a seminar, workshop, or training seminar focusing on racial and ethnic diversity awareness.

References

Bloom, A. (1987). *The closing of the American mind.* New York: Simon Shuster.

Carter, R. (1990, September/October). The relationship between racism and racial identity among white Americans: An exploratory investigation. *The Journal of Counseling and Development,* 69, 46-50.

Gibbs, J.T. (1975). Use of mental health services by black students at a predominantly white university: A three-year study. *American Journal of Ortho-Psychiatry,* 45(3), 430-445.

Giobetti, E., Giobetti, G., Brown, C.; and Smith, R. (1991). Social interaction and multiculturalism. Unpublished studies of black and white students' understanding of multiculturalism.

Livingston, M.S., and Stewart, M.A. (1987). Minority students on a white campus: Perception in truth. *NASPA Journal,* 24(3), 48-51.

Magner, D. (1990, November 14). Amid the diversity racial isolation remains at Berkeley. *The Chronicle of Higher Education,* p. A37-A39.

Muir, D. (1990). A comparison of black and white integration attitudes on a deep south campus: A research note. *Sociological Spectrum,* 10(1), 143-153.

Parker, W.P., and Scott, A.C. (1985). Creating an inviting atmosphere for college students for ethnic minority groups. *Journal of College Student Personnel,* 26(1), 82-87.

Rodriques, E.M. (1989). Racial harassment v. free speech: Policies that avoid legal challenges. *Black Issues in Higher Education,* 2(5), 8-9.

Theodorson, G., and Theodorson, L. (1990). *Sociology.* St. Paul, Minnesota: West Publishing Company.

Zandem, J.W.V. (1987). *Social Psychology.* New York: Random House.

CHAPTER EIGHT

Promoting Diversity and Equity Within California State University
System Level Mandates, Strategies, and Issues

Robbie L. Nayman
James C. Renick
Raymond E. Dye

Expanded access, equity, diversity, and success for underrepresented ethnic groups have become acknowledged goals of American higher education. In pursuit of these goals, many collegiate institutions have accelerated their efforts to recruit, support, and graduate ethnic minority students during the last decade.

The impetus to accelerate efforts to achieve diversity at the nation's colleges and universities has come from a variety of sources. The effects of rapidly changing demographics and unprecedented diversity have created urgent demands on the nation's education system. These forces have prompted state and municipal political leaders, as well as educators, to formulate policies that respond to the new complexities involved in providing universal education to a burgeoning population with diverse needs.

Another force supporting access and equity has come from major regional accreditation associations, which have demonstrated growing sensitivity to the importance of diversity in the academy. Despite some public criticism, regional accrediting associations, such as Western Association of Colleges and Universities and Middle States Accrediting Association, are adjusting their accreditation criteria to include not only student learning outcomes but institutional gains in achieving a multicultural environment. As Howard L. Simmons, executive director of the Commission on Higher Education at the Middle State Association noted, "Accrediting bodies have a duty to look at racial and ethnic climates on campuses in assessing whether the institutions are carrying out their missions" (Leatherman, 1990, p. A12).

Moreover, several states with centralized multicampus postsecondary systems of education have passed legislative mandates to spur the development of master plans to shape and assure the expansion of educational opportunities. Some of the acknowledged leaders of such efforts include California, New York, and Pennsylvania.

While many institutions have successfully accelerated efforts to recruit minority students, faculty, and staff during the last decade, collegiate institutions have experienced less success in the area of retention (Smith, 1989). A growing body of literature (Hively, 1990; Richardson & Skinner, 1991; Carnegie Foundation for the Advancement of Teaching, 1990) concludes that the quality of the campus climate is a decisive factor in effective retention of students, faculty, and staff.

California is often viewed as an important barometer of trends in higher education as they relate to diversity and equity issues. In their book, *Achieving Quality and Diversity* —

Universities in a Multicultural Society, Richardson and Lutomirski (1991) observed, "The California legislature has been a major stimulus for improved opportunities for minorities, establishing its first special higher education programs in 1968'' (p. 151). Hence, the strategies employed by California's educational institutions to promote access, equity, and diversity, and improve campus climate have broad implications for the nation's higher education community and can provide insights potentially useful for other states presently confronting significant multicultural educational issues.

The California State University (CSU) System has adopted the principles of equity and diversity to guide educational and administrative policy, practices, and strategic planning for future growth. The educational equity programs have been designated as the means of implementing this policy, and have been established at each of the 20 campuses that comprise the CSU System.

DIVERSITY AND CAMPUS EQUITY: SOME KEY THEMES

"By the year 2000, (California) will become a majority minority state" (California Commission on the Older, Part-Time Student, 1990, p. 5). California, like the nation itself, will experience accelerated population growth and ethnic diversity. By 2030, the state's population is predicted to be in excess of 32 million (OECD, 1990). In a report from the Joint Committee for Review of the Master Plan for Higher Education (1989), it was pointed out that "early in the 21st century, California will be the first mainland state to attain a majority of nonwhite persons. A third of us will be Latin, a seventh Asian, a twelfth of us Black. All of us will live and work together, building a multicultural society" (p. 1).

Thus, issues of access, equity, diversity, and quality are especially salient for California's educational leadership, in both public and private sectors. The state's demographic profile, with its mosaic of cultural, racial, linguistic, and ethnic groups, mirrors the current complexities and issues confronting American education and forecasts many of the major challenges and opportunities our nation and California face in educating in the 21st century a citizenry unprecedented in its variety of diverse needs. Moreover, a historic tradition of educational opportunity for its citizenry based on the principle of access, equity, and diversity forecast a future of tumultuous challenges for postsecondary higher education.

Policy makers, educators, and students will likely confront many of the salient issues which have been identified in the literature on underrepresented students (Astone & Nunez-Wormack, 1990; Jones & Watson, 1990; Fleming, 1984; Pacarella & Terenzini, 1991; Richardson & Skinner, 1991; Shaw, 1991; Smith, 1989; Gibbs, 1974); and campus climate (Hively, 1990; California State University, 1990; Green, 1988; Carnegie Foundation for the Advancement of Teaching, 1990) in postsecondary education during the last several decades.

Several consistent themes emerged from the body of diversity and equity literature. A common theme contends that an effective infrastructure of academic and student services facilitate the educational success of ethnically diverse students (Green, 1988; Richardson & Skinner, 1991; Jones & Watson, 1990). To be effective, several conditions must be present as part of the support infrastructure. First, support resources must be coordinated between academic affairs and student affairs to facilitate collaborative efforts that support student learning and encourage ongoing institutional commitment.

Second, successful support resources are comprehensive (Reed, 1982) and form a continuum of interrelated services for recruitment, enrollment, retention and graduation. Thus, orientation programs are provided for students and their families or significant others that facilitate preparing for transition from high school to college (Jones & Watson, 1990); academic support services are available that build, develop, and enhance academic competence, such as learning assistance for students who may be underprepared (Jones & Watson, 1990) as well as for students who desire academic enhancement; and assistance is offered to students for whom English is a second language (Suzuki, 1983).

Third, successful support resources offer minority students sufficient opportunities for personal and social skill building development in career and life planning, identity issues, interpersonal skills, and student leadership training. However, Wright (1987) pointed out the necessity for university personnel involved in delivering these services to become sensitized to those unique social and cultural environmental factors specific to minority group students that may affect their receptivity to these services.

Another consistent theme in the diversity and equity literature centers on campus climate and its impact on persistence of minority students in higher education (Christoffel, 1986; Clewell & Ficklen, 1986; Gibbs, 1974; Green, 1988). Campus climate has such saliency because it mirrors quality of life factors that affect the academic performance, developmental growth, and socialization of minority students in the academy. One factor that affects the quality of campus life in California and colleges and universities across the nation is the resurgence of incidents of

racial and ethnic harassment and violence directed at students
who are ethnically and linguistically diverse (Hively, 1990).
In his recent article, "Diversity, Correctness, and Campus
Life," Daniels (1991) estimated that over a million students
and faculty are targets of racial, ethnic, religious, and sexual
slurs scrawled on posters, buildings, and bathroom walls, as
well as vilified in campus newspapers and on radio stations.

Since 1986, racial and ethnic harassment and violent
incidents have been reported at approximately 250 of the
nation's colleges and universities (Ehrlich, 1990). They have
drawn media attention (Slaughter, 1989; Magner, 1989) and
illuminated the threat they pose to the integrity of the
collegiate experience and to the academic community at large.

In response to these disturbing trends, American colleges
and universities have reacted by implementing programs and
policies to address and prevent such conflicts and promote a
greater sense of community. In California, the CSU
chancellor's office convened a panel of educators and lay
citizens to review campus climate system-wide. Their charge
was to access the issues of intolerant behavior, review the
adequacy of existing system policy, and propose
recommendations for system-wide adoption. The panel
produced the document, *Campus Climate — Toward
Appreciating Diversity* (California State University, 1990)
that was forwarded to CSU campuses for implementing the
recommendations. Clearly, the principles of equity and
diversity cannot be successfully implemented through
educational equity programs if campus environments are
marred by incidents of ethnic harassment and violence against
students who are different.

In addition to a supportive campus climate, positive
interaction with a diverse faculty both in and out of class is
another pivotal quality of life factor for diverse students.

Faculty instruction, attitudes, and interaction with students form the core of the academic experience for all students. Concerned faculty involvement in academic advising, mentoring, and participation in campus activities outside the classroom are highly effective contributing factors to student educational success. As pointed out in *Minorities on Campus — A Handbook for Enhancing Diversity,* Green (1988) stated that faculty create the curriculum and determine the quality of the experience in every classroom. They serve as teachers, mentors, advisors, and role models. In a word, faculty are the core of the institution. Without the contributions of minority individuals, no faculty or institution can be complete.

Thus, it is clear that the "campus ecology" of collegiate institutions — all of the environmental characteristics of the institution that affect students — is decisive in its influence, and possesses the ability to enrich or thwart minority students' academic and personal success.

CALIFORNIA'S MASTER PLAN FOR PUBLIC POSTSECONDARY EDUCATION

The state-wide master plan for postsecondary education in California is a composite of public, independent, private, and proprietary schools which encompasses two- and four-year institutions, as well as major research institutions.

The public, state-supported sector is comprised of three distinct "segments," namely: the University of California, with nine campuses; the California State University, with 20 campuses; and the community colleges, with 107 campuses. In the aggregate, these segments represent the largest centralized, multicampus system of its kind in the nation.

The independent sector is comprised of regionally accredited, degree-granting institutions and includes institutions with national reputations, such as Stanford and the California Institution of Technology.

In contrast, private institutions in California refer to nonstate-supported, profit-making entities that are licensed by the state rather than regionally accredited; and can be degree granting or only offer certificates or diplomas (OECD, 1990).

The master plan that directs the state-wide network of postsecondary education in California was adopted formally in 1960 and outlines the missions and responsibilities, entrance requirements, governance, and coordination of the state's three public higher education entities or "inter-segments" (OECD, 1990). To date, the master plan has been reviewed and amended twice since its inception, once during 1972-73 and again during 1985-88. From its origin in 1960 and through successive revisions, the master plan has steadily embodied the goals of access, equity, diversity, and success of underrepresented ethnic groups as central premises of the state's public educational enterprise.

LEGISLATIVE MANDATES

Two legislative mandates were the catalysts for developing equity programs currently at California colleges and universities. The first legislative mandate was Assembly Concurrent Resolution 151 of 1974, which directed the three segments of public higher education — University of California, California State University and community colleges — "prepare a plan that will provide for addressing and overcoming, by 1980, ethnic, sexual, and economic underrepresentation in the makeup of the student bodies of institutions of public higher education" (California Postsecondary Education Commission, 1986, p. 1).

The second legislative mandate, Assembly Concurrent Resolution 83 of 1984, called for "the Regents of the University of California, the Trustees of the California State University, the Board of Governors of California Community Colleges, the Association of Independent Colleges and Universities, the State Board of Education, and the Superintendent of Public Institution to formulate recommendations to assure equal opportunity for low-income state residents to graduate from high school, complete community college, and earn bachelor's degrees" (California Postsecondary Education Commission, 1986, p. 1).

The extent to which the ambitious goals of these mandates are being realized by California's three public segments of higher education is the subject of ongoing and considerable discussion among educators and policy makers across the state. In a later section of this chapter, one segment of public higher education in California — California State University — will be highlighted by examining perceptions of the senior student affairs officers regarding equity issues and programs currently in existence at the 20 campuses that make up the California State University System. Prior to presenting the findings of CSU senior student affair officers' study, a profile of the CSU System is provided below.

CALIFORNIA STATE UNIVERSITY IN PROFILE

California State University is the largest four-year public institution in the country, containing 20 campuses and nine

off-campus centers located throughout the state. Current and
projected campus enrollment for the constituent campuses are
displayed in Table 1.

Table 1
The California State University
Campus Planning Estimates for 2005–06
Campus Enrollment and FTE

Campus	1990–91 Enrollment	FTE	2005–06 Enrollment	FTE
Bakersfield	5,300	3,970	12,000	8,500
Chico	16,000	14,000	16,000	14,000
Dominguez Hills	8,700	6,150	17,000	12,000
Fresno	19,200	16,100	30,500	25,000 *
Fullerton	25,200	17,600	28,600	20,000
Hayward	10,000	8,250	16,700	12,100
Humboldt	7,200	6,760	8,800	8,000
Long Beach	33,300	23,600	35,600	25,000
Los Angeles	20,100	13,550	28,000	18,500
Northridge	29,400	20,900	35,700	25,000
Pomona	18,500	14,700	27,500	19,100
Sacramento	24,700	18,950	31,000	23,400
San Bernardino	10,600	7,750	23,500	17,100 *
San Diego	35,800	25,000	35,800	25,000
San Francisco	27,600	20,000	34,500	25,000 *
San Jose	27,500	20,500	34,700	25,000
San Luis Obispo	16,200	14,700	19,200	17,400 *
San Marcos	400	250	9,700	7,000
Sonoma	7,200	5,400	13,000	10,000
Stanislaus	5,100	3,850	9,500	7,000
Sub-total	348,000	261,980	467,300	344,100
Year-round (summer)	8,000	6,065	15,000	10,900
Off-site instruction			3,600	2,750
Off-campus centers (net)	5,000	3,470	18,000	16,600
Total	361,000	271,515	503,900	374,350

Enrollment estimates based upon student workload factors.
*Requires increase in campus enrollment ceiling.

System-wide enrollment for fall 1990 totaled 369,053 (California State University, 1991). Its oldest campus, San Jose State, was founded in 1857; while the newest campus, San Marcos, accepted its first students in fall 1990.

CSU is governed by a Board of Trustees and chancellor, and is authorized by the master plan to confer the bachelor and masters degrees in all disciplines and for all professions, with the exceptions of law, medicine, veterinary medicine, and dentistry (OECD, 1990). In limited instances, CSU grants joint doctorates with the University of California and with private institutions in the state.

Student Characteristics

The majority of students entering CSU are graduates from California public high schools in the upper one-third of their graduating class, and transfers from California community colleges with a grade point average of 2.0 (California State University, 1991). Through articulation agreements with the California community colleges, CSU serves as a strategic conduit for enabling qualified students to advance from lower-division instruction at a two-year college to upper-division instruction at a four-year institution.

Students at CSU institutions are notably diverse, on several dimensions. They range in age from 12 to 87 years, with an average age of 26. Women comprise slightly over 54 percent of the student population. A sizable number of students enter CSU with previous occupational and professional experience. As of fall 1990, over 53 percent of women were enrolled as part-time, commuter students (California State University, 1991).

With regard to student ethnicity among CSU institutions, 54.2 percent was white non-Latino, according to fall 1990 statistics. Among nonwhite students, 3.3 percent was Filipino; 1.1 percent was American Indian; 12.5 percent was Asian American; 6.0 percent was African American; 0.4 percent was Pacific Islander; 9.3 percent was Mexican American, and 3.3 percent was Other Latino (California State University, 1991).

When viewed within the context of ethnicity, the issues of access, equity, and diversity become especially salient as one observes the number of bachelor's degrees conferred system-wide, depicted in Table 2, compared with the number of bachelor's degrees conferred by CSU institutions to underrepresented groups.

Table 2
CSU Degrees Conferred For 1989-90

Total Degrees Conferred	58,203
Bachelor's	48,326
Master's	9,685
Joint Doctorates	12

Source: Facts About the California State University, April 1991.

Table 3 shows ethnicity by bachelor's degree recipients, as of fall 1990.

Table 3
Bachelor's Degree by Ethnicity for 1989–90

	Number	Percent
African American	1,621	3.7
Native American	444	1.0
Asian American	4,619	10.7
Filipino	941	2.2
Mexican American	2,679	6.2
Other Latino	1,225	2.8
Pacific Islander	173	0.4
All Non-White	11,702	27.0
White Non-Latino	1,632	73.0
Unknown/Nonresident Alien	4,761	9.9

Source: Facts About the California State University, April 1991.

Educational Equity Programs
Educational equity as applied at CSU campuses, refers to equal opportunity, fairness, and impartiality in educational processes that affect underrepresented minorities. Educational equity within CSU has been enunciated as policy that influences funding decisions, educational policies, and administrative practices. The substance of educational equity is to provide vehicles for guaranteeing access and providing retention programs and services that enhance opportunities for underrepresented minority students to succeed.

CSU established its first equity program, the Educational Opportunity Program (EOP), in April 1969. In 1977, a legislative mandate, Assembly Concurrent Resolution 151, assisted CSU in establishing the Student Affirmative Action (SAA) Program. EOP and SAA were pioneer programs in the system's initial educational equity efforts and served as catalysts in developing subsequent additions to system-wide equity programs.

The following are CSU educational equity programs included in the CSU System:

Educational Opportunity Program (EOP)
The program serves low-income and historically underrepresented ethnic students disadvantaged due to educational and economic backgrounds. Under EOP, students are admitted to CSU institutions through both regular admissions and special admissions. It provides comprehensive academic support services, including financial assistance, tutoring, counseling, advising, and summer orientation.

Student Affirmative Action (SAA)
Its original purpose was to extend access and academic support services to underrepresented students eligible for regular admission to CSU. In addition to learning assistance, intensive outreach efforts to high schools and parents by faculty are emphasized.

Trio Programs
Trio includes Special Services for Disadvantaged Students, Talent Search, and Upward Bound. Programs are targeted to low-income and educationally, social, culturally, or physically handicapped students.

Special Services for Disadvantaged Students seeks to increase the academic performance and retention of students. Upward Bound is geared to increase the college-going rate and postsecondary retention of low-income students. Talent Search seeks to reduce high school drop-out rates of low-income disadvantages youth through encouraging them to remain or return to school, and increase the college-going rate of at-risk youth; it provides services to veterans, as well.

Trio Programs offer comprehensive academic support resources, including study skills, tutoring, academic/career counseling, campus visits, increased cultural exposure, admissions and financial aid assistance, and summer transition programs.

Faculty Mentoring
It began as a pilot effort at eight CSU campuses in January 1987. The program encourages faculty-student interaction through a mentoring relationship envisioned to lead to improved academic achievement, retention, and graduation of students from underrepresented ethnic groups. Faculty awareness and improved effectiveness in working with diverse students are additional program goals.

Faculty/Student Mentoring Program (FSMP)
It originated in 1988-89 to parallel efforts of the Faculty Mentoring Program. Its purpose is to test an approach that should enable CSU to reach a large number of minority students needing academic support through student mentors trained by faculty.

Minority Engineering Program (MEP)
MEP increases awareness of career opportunities and support career exploration in engineering for underrepresented students. Activities involve exposure to role models in engineering, enrichment activities, and academic support services. "Incentive" funds encourage campuses to develop and implement activities and programs with high potential for enhancing student retention of Hispanic and African American students.

Retention Incentive Program (RIP)
This program exposes minority females to role models in science and engineering. Its goal is to raise minority females' awareness and aspirations to undertake careers in these fields.

Women in Science and Engineering
This program increases the awareness and interest of minority students in biomedical professions. Emphasis is placed on involving students in collaborative research in biomedical fields to stimulate career exploration in these disciplines.

   The components of the educational equity programs are sufficiently comprehensive to assist students with a continuum of services ranging from early outreach and retention at the high school level through recruitment, financial assistance, and retention at the college level to graduation. Structurally, the educational equity programs contain the features recommended by the literature on equity, diversity, and retention for minority students in higher education.

In the CSU System study discussed in the next section, these educational equity programs are reviewed from the perspective of senior student affairs administrators who are in a position to observe the strengths, weaknesses, and possibilities of equity initiatives at CSU campuses. This study allows the reader to assess the impact of mandated social policy on educational practices at a system level and its progress in increasing the participation of minority students in higher education and contributing to their retention and success.

CALIFORNIA STATE UNIVERSITY SYSTEM STUDY

In spring 1991, California State University (CSU) System senior student affairs officers on each of the 20 campuses comprising the system were sent a questionnaire that focused on educational equity programs. The inquiry was designed to determine the scope of educational equity programs provided; how senior university administrators perceived their effectiveness; receptivity of faculty, administrators, and students to the goals of equity, diversity, and access, as perceived by senior university administrators; sources of dissatisfaction with equity programs by those charged to assist in their implementation; progress towards implementation of system recommendations on improving access and retention/graduation of minority students; and strategies to promote improvement of campus climate with CSU. Sixteen (80 percent) of the 20 student affairs vice presidents responded.

There is an array of educational equity programs in the CSU System that are perceived as having varying degrees of success. As would be assumed, programs related directly to students fall under the student affairs administrative umbrella, and those having to deal primarily with faculty are subsumed under the Office of Academic Affairs.

To assess program effectiveness each respondent was asked to rank the programs on a scale from 1-5, with 5 = Very Effective and 1 = Very Ineffective. The Minority Engineering Program ranked as the most effective program, with the Minority Biomedical Research Support and the Faculty Mentoring Program ranking as the least effective. It must be noted, however, that most programs were ranked in the somewhat effective category or above (See Table 4).

Table 4
Educational Equity Program Currently Available

Program	*N*	*%*	*Effectiveness Rating Mean*
Educational Opportunity Program	16	100	3.78
Student Affirmative Action	16	100	3.78
Trio Programs	12	75	3.88
Faculty Mentoring	11	69	3.44
Minority Engineering Program	11	69	4.23
Faculty/Student Mentoring Program	9	56	3.44
Retention Incentive	5	31	4.00
Women in Science and Engineering	5	31	3.70
Minority Biomedical Research Support	2	13	3.00

Rating Scale
1 = Very Ineffective
5 = Very Effective

The importance attached to equity programs varied by employee category. When asked how faculty, administrators, and students viewed equity programs, the respondents clearly felt that equity matters were more important to administrators than to students or faculty. In fact, the importance they felt faculty attached to the equity effort was substantially lower than students or administrators (see Table 5). This response could be, in part, a function of the administrative role of the respondent. That is, one would assume that an administrator

Table 5
Importance Attached to Equity Programs

Category	Mean Score
Administrators	4.09
Students	3.25
Faculty	2.72

Rating Scale
1=Not Important
5=Very Important

would focus more on the equity administrative aspects. Nevertheless, this finding is consistent with a response in another section of the questionnaire. When asked for a listing of weaknesses of the equity programs currently available on campus, the majority (80 percent) of the respondents listed lack of comprehensive or significant involvement on the part of faculty (See Table 6).

Table 6
Major Program Weaknesses Identified

Weakness	Rank
Faculty Involvement	1
Coordination with Other Programs	2
Assessment of Outcomes	3
Limited Funding	4

Not surprising, when asked to identify important modifications to be made in existing educational equity programs, most respondents mentioned more faculty involvement and coordination as the primary areas where modifications should be made. This theme of limited faculty involvement in the equity domain is a persistent theme that is pervasive. There is a clear perception by senior student affairs officers that faculty have been the least affected by campus equity efforts. This finding is also consistent with earlier assessments of the California system equity report. A 1986 report of the CSU Educational Equity Advisory Council entitled, *Educational Equity in The California State University — Which Way the Future?* (California State University, 1986) recommended increased participation of faculty in equity programs in recognition of limited faculty involvement.

In 1985 an Educational Equity Advisory Council, appointed by the chancellor, conducted a comprehensive review of educational equity programs within the California State University System. Two primary areas identified for improvement were access and retention/graduation. To assess the progress made in responding to these areas, respondents were asked to rate the progress made by rating

1-5, with 1 = Great Progress. Implementation of the access recommendations are perceived as having progressed further than the retention/graduation recommendations (See Tables 7 and 8).

Table 7
Progress Toward 1985 Access Recommendations

Recommendations	Mean Score
Programmatically organize pre-college outreach and community college transfer	2.41
Redefine and restructure outreach/access programs to maximize university activities and increase use of university resources	2.56
Shift resources to outreach activities designed to eliminate the need for admission exceptions	2.84

Rating Scale
1 = Great Progress
5 = Little Progress

Table 8
Progress Toward 1985 Retention/Graduation Recommendations

Recommendations	Mean Score
Develop a mandatory orientation program for all first-time students and transfers	2.75
Develop a computer data base for students admitted under special categories and students considered to have potential problems	3.03
Establish an "early warning" system to monitor the academic progress of students and follow-up on students with academic problems	3.03
Develop goals, standards and objectives to evaluate persistence and graduation rates for underrepresented students and the effectiveness of campus educational equity efforts.	2.70

Rating Scale
1 = Great Progress
5 = Little Progress

A surprising finding is the low percentage of student affairs vice presidents who have formally discussed the 1990 publication, *Campus Climate: Toward Appreciating Diversity* (California State University, 1990), issued by the chancellor's office. This report on campus climate prepared by a panel of experts, was broadly distributed throughout the CSU System. Only 44 percent of the vice presidents had formally discussed the document. Not surprisingly, administrators who discussed the document attached more significance to the document than those who had not discussed it.

The scope and variety of equity activities initiated at CSU campuses within the last year are illustrated in Table 9. They reflect a proactive, preventive approach to diversity programming, as opposed to reactive measures.

Table 9
Equity Activities Initiated on Campus within the Last Year

Activity	% of Campuses that Initiated Activity
Special events to celebrate different cultures and promote cultural diversity	100
To promote multicultural diversity	95
Measures to prevent and/or respond to bias-related incidents	75
Courses in the academic curriculum to promote cultural diversity	69
Policy statement endorsing or reaffirming adherence to diversity, civility and community	50

CONCLUSION

National discourse on the effects of an increasingly diverse society and the need to ensure the productive use of all human resources have created significantly policy initiatives and government mandates. These policies are, in large measure, outgrowth of the earlier 1960s civil rights movement. Universities and colleges have been important participants in policy development, as well as in policy debates. Not unlike the campus civil rights activities of the '60s, the various "remedies" or "solutions" have had varying degrees of success. The current forms of campus-based civil rights, namely multicultural diversity and campus climate issues, have focused primarily on the four fundamental dimensions of recruitment or access, campus climate, retention, and graduation rates.

Public policy within California has created an array of campus-based programs designed to enhance the educational experience of students within the CSU System by supporting diversity initiatives. Indeed, public policy has established equity and diversity as basic premises that anchor educational structure, distribution of financial resources, and programmatic priorities.

While the infrastructure of the educational equity programs at CSU campuses conform to programmatic requisites suggested by the literature on equity and diversity, African American and other ethnic minority students remain underrepresented within CSU. This finding was consistent with earlier findings from the 1985 comprehensive review of the CSU equity programs commissioned by the chancellor's office. In that study, access and retention/graduation rates were identified as major issues for the system.

Underrepresentation of minority students at CSU campuses is exacerbated by the three areas perceived by key administrators as major constraints to successful equity programs within CSU, namely, slow progress toward implementation of recommendations on access, retention and graduation; lack of significant involvement of faculty in equity programs; and uneven coordination of equity programs with other campus support resources.

Moreover, like much of higher education, California is facing budget cuts that threaten the well-being of postsecondary education at every level. Preoccupation with budget and program downsizing, increased work loads, and diminished employee morale pose precedented challenges to collegiate institutions and their ability to address the very issues that most influence the likelihood of minority students gaining access to higher education and receiving a quality education, namely, committed faculty working with administrators to provide opportunities for student learning and success.

The inherent soundness and desirability of educational equity programs within CSU persist, despite real issues in the need of redress. Although uneven in its implementation, educational equity policy will contribute to increased participation of minority students in higher education at CSU campuses and help shape California's future higher education institutions so that they continue to espouse diversity, equity, and access as operating premises and develop effective paradigms for their implementation.

This CSU study provides an important example of the implementation of public policy through a series of legislative mandates and campus commitments. Campus administrative leadership has responded by designing numerous programs and events to enhance multicultural diversity and campus climate. Numerous recommendations and mandates have been pursued. Other states can assess the effectiveness of the courses pursued as the CSU System implements its equity and diversity mandates within institutions that offer campus environments which challenge, support, and enrich the lives of all its inhabitants.

References

Astone, B., and Nunez-Wormack, E. (1990). *Pursuing diversity: Recruiting college minority students.* (ASHE-ERIC Higher Education Report No. 7.) Washington, D.C.: ASHE-ERIC Clearinghouse on Higher Education.

California Commission on the Older, Part-time Student. (1990). *Policies and practices to meet the needs of older, part-time students.* Long Beach, California: California State University.

California Postsecondary Education Commission. (1986). *Background for expanding educational equity — A technical supplement to the report of the intersegmental policy task force on assembly concurrent resolution 83.* Sacramento: author.

California State University, (1986). *Educational equity in the California state university — Which way the future?* Long Beach: author.

California State University (1990). *Campus climate — Toward appreciating diversity.* A report prepared for the California State University by the Panel of Experts on Campus Climate. Long Beach: author.

California Student University (1991). *Facts about the California State University.* Long Beach: author.

Carnegie Foundation for the Advancement of Teaching (1990). *Campus life — In search of community.* Princeton, N.J.: author.

Christoffel, P. (1986, October). *Minority student access and retention: A review.* New York: The College Board.

Clewell, B.C., and Ficklen, M.S. (1986). *Improving minority retention in higher education: A search for effective institutional practices.* Princeton, N.J.: Educational Testing Service.

Daniels, L.A. (1991). Diversity, correctness and campus life. *Change,* 23(5), 16-20.

Ehrlich, H.J. (1990, March). *Campus ethnoviolence and the policy options.* (Institute Report No. 4.) Baltimore, Maryland: National Institute Against Prejudice and Violence.

Fleming, J. (1984). *Blacks in college: A comparative study of students' success in black and white institutions.* San Francisco: Jossey-Bass.

Gibbs, J.T. (1974). Patterns of adaptation among black students at a predominantly white university. *American Journal of Orthopsychiatry,* 44, 728-740.

Green, M.F. (1988). *Minorities on campus — A handbook for enhancing diversity.* Washington, D.C.: American Council on Education.

Hively, R. (1990). *The lurking evil: Racial and ethnic conflict on the college campus.* Washington, D.C.: American Association of State Colleges and Universities.

Joint Committee for Review of the Master Plan for Higher Education (1989). *California faces . . . California's future:*

Education for citizenship in a multicultural democracy.
Sacramento: California Legislature.

Jones, D.J., and Watson, B.C. (1990). *High risk students and higher education: Future trends.* (ASHE-ERIC Higher Education Report No. 3.) Washington, D.C.: ERIC Clearinghouse on Education.

Leatherman, C. (1990, August 15). 2 of 6 regional accrediting agencies take steps to prod colleges on racial, ethnic diversity. *The Chronicle of Higher Education*, p. A12.

Magner, D.K. (1989, April 26). Blacks and whites on the campuses: Behind ugly racist incidents, student isolation and insensitivity. *The Chronicle of Higher Education*, p. A1.

Organization for Economic Co-Operation and Development (OECD) (1990). *Reviews of national policies for education on higher education in California.* Paris, France: author.

Pascarella, E.T., and Terenzini, P.T. (1991). *How colleges affect students — Findings and insights from twenty years of research.* San Francisco: Jossey-Bass.

Reed, S. (1982). *TRIO/special services program evaluation.* Minneapolis: University of Minnesota General College.

Richardson, R.C., Jr., and Lutomirski, P.N. (1992). University of California, Los Angeles. In R.C. Richardson, Jr., and E.F. Skinner, *Achieving quality and diversity — Universities in a multicultural society.* New York: Macmillan Publishing.

Richardson, R.C., Jr., and Skinner, E.F. (1991). *Achieving quality and diversity — Universities in a multicultural society.* New York: Macmillan Publishing.

Slaughter, J.B. (1989, October 7). Bigotry is back in fashion: Many forms of racism infest nation's campuses. *The Los Angeles Times*, p. 7.

Smith, D. (1989). *The challenge of diversity: Involvement or alienation in the academy?* (ASHE-ERIC Report No. 5). Washington, D.C.: ASHE-ERIC Clearinghouse on Education.

Suzuki, B.H. (1983). The education of Asian and Pacific Americans: An introductory overview. In D.T. Nakanishi and M. Hirano-Nakanishi (Eds.), *The education of Asian and Pacific Americans: Historical perspectives and prescriptions for the future.* Phoenix: Oryx Press.

Wright, D.J. (1987). Minority students: Developmental beginnings. In D.J. Wright (Ed.), *Responding to the needs of today's minority students.* San Francisco: Jossey-Bass.

CHAPTER NINE

Global Diversity and Student Development
Educating for World Citizenship

Marvalene Hughes

It is commonly observed that campuses are becoming increasingly diverse, and the world is a much smaller place. Have theories of human development and educational practice kept pace with these changes?

The need for a utilitarian paradigm in global and domestic multicultural education which broadens perspectives beyond circumscribed views becomes evident when one examines the deficiencies of current practices. Drawn together by satellite communication, citizens world-wide have the opportunity to become members of a "global community" which does not require homogeneous views to co-exist. International travel is a *sine qua non,* and governments, economies, and markets have become more integrated and interdependent. One factor which contributes to the campus as a global community is the projection that at least 10 percent of our students will spend a minimum of one semester in another country. An outgrowth of these trends will be required multilingual and multicultural competencies.

As a result of this recently acknowledged interdependence, changes and events in one part of the "community" often have profound effects in other parts. Conspicuous examples include the tumbling of the Berlin Wall, the collapse of the Soviet Union, and the slow dismantling of apartheid in South Africa. These events have had great impact on political and economic issues. The often unpredictable political and social upheavals of the last few years have thus not been isolated events to be studied from afar, but rather have resulted in shock waves felt around the world. A poignant example of this fact was the construction, during the Tianamen Square crisis, of a huge replica of the sculpture of "Liberty" by a coalition of Chinese and American students on the University of Minnesota campus and of how it galvanized public opinion in the United States.

Recent trends suggest the importance of a new global diversity paradigm. Among these trends are major population movements, other unpredicted and unpredictable circumstances world-wide, and domestic demographic shifts.

DOMESTIC DEMOGRAPHIC SHIFTS

Over the past decade, demographers in the United States have alerted us to the changing patterns of populations which bring into sharp focus several important trends for higher education. Of particular interest are increases in populations of students of color, increases in nontraditional students, and increases in the female population which resulted in a larger ratio of female to male students on campuses.

By 1990, minorities of all ages will constitute 20-25 percent of our total population, while their percentage among youth cohorts will be over 30 percent (it is 26 percent today). In some states, particularly Texas and California, minorities will be over 45 percent of the state birth cohort (Hodgkinson, 1983, p. 15).

The American Council on Education (1988) reinforced this dramatic shift by documenting that one-third of our nation is comprised of people of color. Other population trends affecting student development in the United States are:

❐ An expanding population of those over 65 years

❐ An increase in the 34-44 year age group among students

❐ An expanding Asian and Hispanic population

❐ An increase in the number of African American women in education, while the number of African American men declined

❐ A growing consciousness of the need to better serve the disabled, those who represent diversity in religious affiliations, and the growing population of "out-of-the-closet" lesbians, gays, and bisexuals.

IMMIGRATION AND INTERNATIONAL STUDIES

Data on immigration and naturalization reveal marked population shifts. In 1989, the United States admitted 1,090,924 immigrants as compared to 460,348 in 1979. The 1989 immigrants came from Europe (82,891), Asia

(312,149), Africa (25,166), Oceania (4,360), North America (a total of 607,398 of which 405,172 were from Mexico), the Caribbean (88,982), Central America (101,034), and South America (58,926) (Zikopoulos, 1990).

International study has increased opportunities for global interaction among the student populations of the world. There have been numerous social spin-offs. For example, many international students have host families in the United States and in other countries, and institutions and organizations often sponsor local events which facilitate social interaction among locals and internationals. These are examples of increasing efforts to reduce marginalization of international students.

Enrollment of international students in universities within the United States increased rapidly. Asian students grew by leaps and bounds in the United States. Over 40 percent (four of six) international undergraduate students in the United States were from Asia while 60 percent of the graduate international students were Asian (Zikopoulos, 1988). The majority of the students from India (82.5 percent), Canada (81.5 percent), Japan (79.2 percent), China (78.7 percent) and the Republic of Korea (69.8 percent) enroll in universities in the United States (Zikopoulos, 1990).

International students in higher education are an important barometer of the new global interdependence. Statistics indicate that foreign study is increasing and that more countries are serving as hosts for students from other countries. According to the *UNESCO Statistical Yearbook* (1989), 118 countries served as hosts in their higher education institutions for 1,091,766 international students; an increase of 1.2 percent over 1988. UNESCO also reported that Europe was host to the largest foreign student population (76 percent, or 446,497), while North America, mainly the United States, followed. When disaggregated by country instead of region, the United States was by far the largest receiving country for foreign student enrollment (386,851), followed by France (123,978), Germany (81,724), and the United Kingdom (53,694) (Zikopoulos, 1990). On balance, the international student matriculation pattern in the United States has remained proportional to the student population in higher education. For example, in 1954-55, the percentage of foreign students in the U.S. was 1.4 percent as compared to 2.8 percent in 1984 (Zikopoulos, 1988). There are well over 12 million students in postsecondary education in the United States; including 386,851 international students who continue to comprise less than 3 percent of the total. Most foreign students from the United States studied in the Federal Republic of Germany (20.3 percent), the United Kingdom (19.9 percent), France (16.6 percent), and Canada (12.8 percent) (Zikopoulos, 1990). These international trends, coupled with increasing domestic diversity, signify the need for education to expand the classroom and student development curriculum to include training for world citizenship.

EDUCATION FOR WORLD CITIZENSHIP

Newell and Davis (1988) identified six principles which they viewed as essential requirements for 21st century citizenship. They charged educators with the responsibility to involve students in experiences, research, and services to acquire the following skills:

1. Civic literacy is the education of citizens to understand not only "complex societal issues such as nuclear weapons, acid rain,

poverty, and genetic engineering, but to make informed moral, economic, political and scientific judgements about them . . . " (p. 29).

2. Critical thinking enables citizens to go beyond understanding and analyzing political issues to become spokespersons who think critically and question authority.

3. Social conscience focuses citizens' actions and thinking on the identification of common goals and works to remediate the "heartless society."

4. Tolerating and respecting diversity is an essential requirement in a world where over seven-eighths of the citizens are nonwhite. The need to move beyond tolerance to understanding and appreciation is underscored.

5. Global citizenship calls upon everyone to realize the interdependence of all international, national, and local actions. The ozone layer and the greenhouse effect, for example, are interdependent phenomena.

6. Political action translates good intentions and knowledge into action and involvement.

Newell and Davis (1988) concluded that student involvement in campus leadership and off-campus political activities should be encouraged through interdisciplinary general education courses.

STUDENT DEVELOPMENT THEORIES

It is clear from the foregoing sketch of domestic and international change that there are important ramifications and challenges for the student affairs and student development professional. The concept of the "global community" no longer can be a glib cliche but must become an increasingly accurate metaphor for an ever-pressing reality. Domestic demographic data and statistics on immigration and world-wide student mobility have illuminated the environment in which we now live, study, and work. We can see in the mirror of fact the true nature of our evolving human community.

Within the context of this new interglobal world, what sources can we draw upon to inform educational practitioners in the coming years? It is evident that student development theory and diversity education will need to reflect a more multidisciplinary approach, informed by studies in sociology, demography, ethnography, cultural and social anthropology, group psychology, and history. An apparent limitation of much of contemporary student development research is its almost exclusive focus on individual development and behavior.

Several theories can be augmented to include consideration of cultural development. For example, Chickering (1969) introduced seven "vectors" to describe college student development: developing competence, managing emotions, developing autonomy, establishing identity, freeing interpersonal relations, clarifying purpose, and developing integrity.

These competencies, which students struggle to master in college, can also be defined in a broader cultural context. What constitutes autonomy or identity, for example, may vary from culture to culture. Hughes (1987), for example, found that achieving "individuation among Black students represents an interdependent family dimension that ensures continuing contact with family, respect for parental authority, respect for aging persons, and respect for the Black community" (p. 540). Hughes (1987) believed this interdependent pattern of individuation is representative of the Afrocentric culture which promulgates the value of the extended family.

Other research has also challenged traditional student development notions, such as the assumption that personal development can be understood apart from community and group identity (Hughes, 1987). Gilligan (1982) recognized the limitations of Lawrence Kohlberg's work in moral development and thereby achieved a profound breakthrough in documenting significant differences in women's moral developmental patterns. Gilligan (1982) found affiliation to be a central element early on in women's development.

A pressing question raised by internationalization is the role of spiritual development in personal growth. Hughes (1983) encouraged educators to augment the standard set of student development goals to include spiritual and cultural development. If interpreted narrowly, the first of these goals may seem problematic to educators understandably wary of transgressing the boundaries between church and state. Interpreted more broadly, however, and not with reference to any particular religious orientation, spirituality may be quite appropriately understood as a significant part of the human experience. Some international cultures include spiritual identity as central to cultural identity. In the United States, this is also true for the Native American and African American cultures. Despite growing evidence of the centrality of cultural development (associated with racial, ethnic, cultural, and other differences), cultural identity is a phenomenon not yet fully integrated within education. Cultural development as a goal in student development lays the foundation for multicultural values and global diversity.

STAGES OF MULTICULTURAL DEVELOPMENT

Studies in identity development typically conclude that individuals' readiness for diversity can be described in stages. For purposes of this study, Jefferson's (1988) stages were summarized as follows:

Stage One: Isolate Stage. Typically persons in this stage identify with their own group and assert the superiority of that group.

Stage 2: Inquiry Stage. In programming, the needs and tastes of the majority culture remain the central focus; persons may acknowledge the existence of other cultures.

Stage 3: Contact Stage. In this stage tolerance of diversity is achieved but full acceptance is not attained.

Stage 4: Integration Stage. People in this stage celebrate and speak out for diversity.

Is it enough to celebrate and speak out for diversity or is there a stage where humanity concurrently endorses and reinforces diversity while reaching for universal values of humanity? Should we transcend our differences to attain the highest level of human development? Are there universal principles and values? This study sought answers to these questions.

Research Method

Ethnography as a naturalistic, qualitative research methodology has gained increased visibility in the last few years. The increasing acceptance of this method of inquiry parallels the growing research on diversity and global awareness. It enables researchers to study group interactions and interpret the "meanings" of differing behavioral patterns and cultural norms. As such, it is instructive for researchers in student development, particularly as movement is made toward intergroup and global world view perspectives on campus. "Many of the tenets of ethnography derive from a philosophical position sometimes referred to as *interpretivism* that is quite different from the logical positivism underlying traditional educational research" (Eisenhart, 1988, p. 102). Interpretivism invites the researcher to be a participant who makes meaning out of observations and dialogue. Traditionally, it has been associated with anthropologists who endeavor to study the totality of the human experience. Eisenhart (1988) described four ethnographic methodologies:

   ❐ "Participant observation is the ethnographer's major technique
   for being both involved in and detached from the topic of study"
   (p. 105). It calls upon the researcher to understand and integrate
   the experience empathically — observing with innocent eyes, ears,
   taste, touch, and sound, while becoming immersed in the
   experience of the observed.

   ❐ Ethnographic interviewing enables the ethnographer to discover
   the participants' subjective views. Interviews may be formally

structured or they may be informal, but they generally ask
open-ended questions. This process is extremely time consuming.

❐ The search for artifacts allows the researcher to collect materials,
written documents, or graphics which relate to the participants
under study.

❐ Researcher introspection engages the researcher in a reflection
which may produce emotional responses, expanded interpretations,
or insights.

Data Collection
In this study, three methods were employed: (1) participant
observation, (2) ethnographic interviewing, and (3)
researcher introspection. The study began in 1984 in the
form of a workshop in Johannesburg and Soweto, South
Africa. Observing the oppressive human conditions of
apartheid stimulated an inquiry regarding principles and
values which were universal irrespective of the social,
economic, and political conditions of society. Groups and
individuals in South Africa were asked the following
questions: What do you believe your birthright to be? If you
could describe the most important birthrights or entitlements
for yourself and humankind all over the world, what would
they be?
   During the two-week workshop in South Africa, two of
the nine principles discussed in this chapter were identified:
personal development and human rights, although at the time
they were labelled freedom to become educated, to live where
one wishes, and to marry whomever one chooses.

Participants emphasized the right to become educated, the right to worship, and the importance of freedom. Since then the same questions have been posed to participants from the following countries: Argentina, Australia, Austria, the Bahamas, Canada, the Caribbean, Chile, China, Colombia, Costa Rica, Czechoslavakia, El Salvador, Germany (East and West), Hungary, Iceland, India, Israel, Japan, Lithuania, Mexico, Nicaragua, Nigeria, Philippines, Poland, Portugal, Russia, Singapore, Spain, South Africa, Sweden, Switzerland, United Arab Emirates, Venezuela, the United Kingdom, United States, and West Africa. Large- and small-group interviews were conducted through workshops and group encounters. Individual interviews were also conducted in some countries.

Workshops were facilitated in the United States to validate initial findings. Most notably, the workshop was featured at

Table 1
Nine Universal Human Values

Personal Development Entitlements
- Development of human potential through educational opportunity
- Freedom to define one's own spiritual path
- Privileges to enjoy a high quality of life to include nutrition, lifestyle choices, health care planning, health education, and wellness

Human Rights and Dignity
- Preservation of the rights of all peoples, as groups with cultural identities and as individuals with transcendent human rights

Self-Determination and Free Election
- Opportunities to determine one's individual destiny (micro) and to engage in free elections (macro)

Global Economic Arrangements
- Economic interdependence and well-being as a counter to ethnocentric and geopolitical greed

Ecological Well-Being
- Global arrangements to preserve the environment and planet

Technological Interdependence
- Appropriate world development through shared resources, particularly for underdeveloped countries

Global Political Understandings
- Paradigms of power and politics to promote collaboration around the globe, transcend geopolitical ideologies, and prevent conflict from escalating into violence

Global Security
- Increased efforts to build a "trusting" and peaceful world instead of a nuclear world, a world free of violence domestically and internationally

World Order
- The development of global conduct and ethical codes to govern the human condition

the national conference of the American Association of Counseling and Development in Cincinnati in March 1990, where approximately 300 participants critiqued and discussed the nine universal human values presented in this chapter for three hours. The final sessions were convened at the University of Minnesota during the summer, 1991, meeting of the International Counseling Institute, attended by representatives from 12 countries, followed by a critique from two classes of graduate students at the University of Minnesota during the 1991-92 academic year.

Results

Results were analyzed by engaging participants in: (1) identifying themes in workshops and (2) reacting to themes identified in other settings. Critiques were made of tapes, journals, written and verbal evaluations of sessions, and written correspondence. In all sessions the themes which had been identified previously were described. Participants were asked to discuss them and make additional recommendations for clarification and universality. In London, for example, there was an overwhelming consensus that spirituality should be made an explicit dimension of personal development. The international participants at the University of Minnesota conference endorsed all of the nine principles in Table 1. The additional problem identified by the Minnesota participants related to the challenge that we all face in ensuring that individuals and groups gain access to the kinds of experiences needed to attain the Universal Human Values.

Research from national and international sessions revealed nine values which were identified to be transformative world view values (see Table 1). These themes were derived from workshops and groups conducted with world leaders, academicians, politicians, student affairs professionals, human service providers, volunteers, actors/actresses, and citizens from 36 countries. These values were described as human entitlements or birthrights. They constitute goals toward which all societies should aspire, despite their cultural, religious, familial, or political beliefs. These nine values encapsulate principles which participants viewed as universal or global world views.

Table 2 lists seven stages, resulting from this study, which humankind must master to achieve transformation. Individually and collectively these stages must be mastered by world citizens seeking to promote a global society.

Education is the key to change. One either grows toward transformation or regresses to complacency. Table 2, Channels of Diversity: Challenging Complacency, was developed as an educational model which charges educators with the responsibility to challenge complacency. It identifies those stages which individuals must master to transcend prejudice due to socialization. The last stage, transformation, is achieved when the nine universal values become a reality for all humankind. This represents a new stage in the research on student development. The addition of a new substage of "openness to change" gives credence to the often strong emotional encounters experienced by individuals who risk challenging their complacency. Fear, guilt, anger, confusion and rage may trigger denial and resistance. On the other hand, persons who understand that the pain accompanying these emotions could signal a growth transition may be inspired to advance to the stage of acceptance.

Table 2

Channels of Diversity:
Challenging Complacency

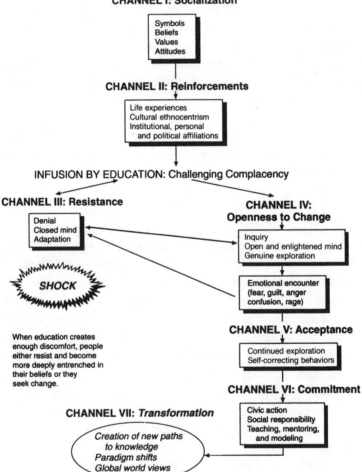

CHANNEL I: Socialization

Symbols
Beliefs
Values
Attitudes

CHANNEL II: Reinforcements

Life experiences
Cultural ethnocentrism
Institutional, personal
    and political affiliations

INFUSION BY EDUCATION: Challenging Complacency

CHANNEL III: Resistance

Denial
Closed mind
Adaptation

SHOCK

When education creates
enough discomfort, people
either resist and become
more deeply entrenched in
their beliefs or they
seek change.

CHANNEL IV:
Openness to Change

Inquiry
Open and enlightened mind
Genuine exploration

Emotional encounter
(fear, guilt, anger
confusion, rage)

CHANNEL V: Acceptance

Continued exploration
Self-correcting behaviors

CHANNEL VI: Commitment

Civic action
Social responsibility
Teaching, mentoring,
    and modeling

CHANNEL VII: *Transformation*

*Creation of new paths
to knowledge
Paradigm shifts
Global world views*

Implications

As society and its institutions struggle to manage the challenges of diversity, educators debate the perceived distinction between excellence and diversity. Meanwhile, students in higher education experience frustration and confusion regarding the values and goals of diversity. Are professionals trained and prepared to address diversity? What is the significance and meaning of the debate over whether diversity affects quality and excellence?

In the educational market place the terms *excellence* and *diversity* are really synonymous. Bernstein (1990) stated:

> Colleges and universities must embrace diversity because their survival as centers of excellence and democracy-enhancing institutions depends on it (p. 19).

Accordingly, excellence in a diverse world cannot be attained without diversity. Certainly, the basic precepts of world citizenship education are dependent on success in creating diverse communities.

Higher education will be fundamentally different as it aspires to create an academic climate which fosters domestic diversity and world citizenship education. New opportunities presented by world citizenship education include:

> ❏ When the world becomes an open market place, there will be increased mobility among faculty, staff, students, and administrators as training and qualifications are recognized transnationally.

> ❏ Unless preventive steps are taken, the lower socioeconomic class in the United States and in the world at large will be deprived of

many of the privileges of education, particularly, the privilege of international education to become world citizens.

❏ The curriculum will need to be reshaped in early education, specifically in relation to languages and cultures thus affecting preparation requirements of prospective students in higher education.

❏ Shared research among universities in the global community will open up new opportunities for professors around the globe.

❏ The goal of diversity will become a global world view.

❏ Global multiculturalism will escalate tension and conflict largely due to unresolved domestic diversity. New modes of mediation and conflict management will become central to student affairs.

❏ Global communities unaccustomed to first amendment rights will endure initial strain as students and faculty test the boundaries of democracy.

❏ Democratization and the responsibilities to teach, without indoctrinating, will become an ever-pressing issue in environments which resist democracy.

TRAINING STUDENTS TO BE STEWARDS

Restructuring leadership development training for students may be an appropriate beginning. When we train leaders today we risk falling into the tradition of an authority model, not integrating the profound learnings from other cultural leadership paradigms. New leadership is needed which promotes values of stewardship. Stewardship means that we teach people to care about and respect one another, to learn to value interdependence, and to care about community building in our university, our country and our global community.

When efforts to promote diversity create unrest, students need, more than ever, to receive training in stewardship. Stewards care about the welfare of others deeply and are invested in preserving the universe for the good of the future society. Stewards operate on those nine transcendent values in Table 1 which enable them to subjugate their concerns about personal gains to focus on the good of society. Stewards are transcendent in their purpose and vision. A course in stewardship would include strategies to empower students to manage conflict and develop empathic understandings.

Stewardship will define for the future society:

❐ A new reality which honors diversity.

❐ A noble mission to serve humanity.

❐ A commitment to empathic communication.

❐ A global commitment to build community, surrender independence, and overcome greed and individuality.

❐ An endorsement of values of inclusivity.

❐ A community building vision of a possible future which can offer a combination of a productive, creative, healthy and joyful local and global community.

❒ A strategy of hope for those who struggle to survive in a world of politics and plenty.

❒ A form of leadership where leaders take strength and energy from followers and vice versa.

Characteristics of the good steward include:

❒ People committed to a mission to do good for people. They understand that nothing we live to enjoy can be safe for us until we make it available to everyone.

❒ Individuals who live their lives empathically.

❒ People who care about people.

❒ People who place compassion, integrity, and the welfare of others uppermost in their value structure.

❒ People who care about the future generations and the future of our planet.

An example of global stewardship is the Peace Corps. Programs on campuses which represent these values include Campus Outreach Opportunity League (COOL), "Into the Streets," and the resurgence of student community service efforts.

NEW SKILLS FOR THE
STUDENT AFFAIRS PROFESSIONAL

Student affairs professionals will need to acquire new skills to understand and institute student development in the global community. Essential student affairs skills will include:

☐ Building authentic community. Hughes (1988) suggested we turn to education to create strategies to build an authentic human community: "The true human community must address deeper human values and attitudes to guarantee that humanity will strive for and attain the highest level of human maturity" (p. 1). This suggests we must go beyond singing the same songs and eating the same foods in our campus community building initiatives. The Carnegie Foundation for the Advancement of Teaching (1990) identified six components of community building: (1) purposeful education, (2) open climate, (3) just environment, (4) caring environment, (5) disciplined environment, and (6) celebrative community.

☐ Teaching conflict management and mediation skills. Conflict among multicultures is inevitable and constructive. Conflict resolution is central to diversity training. Professionals could benefit greatly by enhancing their multicultural conflict resolution skills.

☐ Preserving cultures through purposeful educational planning. Education which honors diversity will demand preservation of cultures and pluralistic teachings. This view will not be perceived as displacing nor denigrating another.

☐ Forging compatibility between human development and advancements in technology. Technology has advanced at a pace which is more rapid than humankind has been able to assimilate. Thus, attitudes and beliefs lag behind our technological preparation to engage with other societies.

❐ Teaching care for our environment. We must learn to care for our planet, using energy preservation and efficient waste management. We need to rediscover the secrets and joys of protecting the earth. We must value protecting and replenishing the earth's natural resources.

❐ Mobilizing people and resources for global understanding. Citizens and, in some instances, organizational resources are available to promote global interaction and understanding.

❐ Managing social problems on campus. Since our campuses are microcosms of society, it follows that societal problems will be mirrored on campus. Our preparation must therefore be broad enough to manage societally originated situations.

❐ Becoming forecasters for education. Education receives the future generation at impressionable periods, whether at 18 or 81. We are in the business of "educating" the future society in formative periods, and we need to forecast, interpret, and integrate new learnings about diversity in ways which faculty and administration can understand and support.

CONCLUSION

Even as you read, the world is shrinking and changing. Diversity has become an international reality. Given the scarcity of research on global diversity, it follows that our knowledge of universal human values is not sufficient to equip us for the enormous challenges associated with our rapid international changes. As professionals we must prepare ourselves to respond actively, drawing upon the research and experience available in the field and pushing beyond. We have yet to master domestic (U S.) diversity, but it is abundantly clear that student affairs professionals and students must develop world citizenship competencies. We can no longer rely on demands of pressure groups forging their agenda which often yields symptomatic responses in lieu of systemic multicultural student development which preserves the richness of diversity and honors the nine universal human values. A systemic approach will take into account the nine universal values identified in this chapter and begin to channel researchers toward global student development, world citizenship education, and transformation.

References

American Council on Education. (1988). *One-third of a nation.* Washington, D.C.: author.

Bernstein, A. (1990, March/April). Sex, race, and diversity tapes: Students on campus. *Change*, 18, 23.

Carnegie Foundation for the Advacement of Teaching. (1990). *Campus life: In search of community.* Princeton, N.J.: author.

Chickering, A. (1969). *Education and identity.* San Francisco: Jossey-Bass.

Eisenhart, M. (1988). The ethnographic research tradition and mathematic education research. *Journal for Research in Mathematics Education*, 19, 99-114.

Gilligan, C. (1982). *In a different voice: Psychological theory and women's development.* Cambridge: Harvard University Press.

Hodgkinson, H.L. (1983, March/April) Guess who's coming to college. *Academe*, 13-20.

Hughes M. (1983). Effective models of systematic program planning. In M. Barr and L. Keating, *Developing effective student services programs* (pp. 181-211). San Francisco: Jossey-Bass.

Hughes, M. (1987). Black students' participation in higher education. *Journal of College Student Personnel*, 28, 532.

Hughes, M. (1988). Building a human community: A mission of education and student affairs. *ACPA Developments*, XV.

Jefferson, F.C. (1988, March). Training develops multicultural awareness. *ACU-I Bulletin*, 12-16.

Newell, W.H., and Davis, A.J. (1988). Education for citizenship: The role of progressive education and interdisciplinary studies. *Innovative Higher Education*, 13.

UNESCO. (1989). *Statistical yearbook 1989*. New York: author.

Zikopoulos, M, (Ed.). (1988). *Open doors: 1987/88 report on international educational exchange.* New York: Institute of International Education.

Zikopoulos, M. (Ed.). (1990). *Open doors: 1989/90 report on international educational exchange.* New York: Institute of International Education.

Appendix A

Recommended Reading

Carter, D.J., and Wilson, R. (1991). *Minorities in higher education. Ninth annual status report.* Washington, D.C.: American Council on Education.

Commission for the Review of the Master Plan (1987). *The master plan renewed: Unity, equity, quality, and efficiency in California postsecondary education.* Sacramento: author.

DePree, M. (1989). *Leadership is an art.* New York: Dell Publishing.

Dervarics, C. (1988, October 13). Discrimination still a barrier to success, say black students in Oberlin study. *Black Issues in Higher Education,* p. 4.

Galligani, D.J. (1984, April). Changing the culture of the university. Paper presented at the annual meeting of the American Educational Research Association, New Orleans.

Greene, E. (1989, April 26). At Oberlin: Liberal traditions, intentions are no guarantee of racial harmony. *The Chronicle of Higher Education,* p. A31.

Guthrie, V.L., Friedlander, W., Gilderbloom, J.G., Henderson, M., Wishnia, G., Bucholtz, G., Israel, S., Collins, D.A., Burayidi, M., Thompson, S., Bailey, P., Golden, D.J., Parrott, D.W., King, K., McMullian, M., Buchter, M., Wagner, S.L., Campeau, F., and Golden, D.C. (1990). Attitudes and reactions to University of Louisville's celebration of diversity program.

Unpublished report, University of Louisville, School of Urban Policy.

Jones, A.C., Terrell, M.C., and Duggar, M.H. (1991, Winter). The role of student affairs in fostering cultural diversity in higher education. *NASPA Journal,* 28(2), 121-127.

King, L.R. (1986, February). Cultural diversity: New directions for education. Paper presented at a meeting of the National Social Science Association, Seattle.

Kuh, G.D., Schuh, J.H., Whitt, E.J., and Associates. (1991). *Involving colleges — Successful approaches to fostering student learning and development outside the classroom.* San Francisco: Jossey-Bass.

Lenning, O.T., and Nayman, R.L. (Eds.). (1980). *New roles in learning assistance.* San Francisco: Jossey-Bass.

Leo, J. (1990, January 8). Racism on American college campuses. *U.S. News & World Report,* p. 53.

Leppo, J. (1987). Multicultural programming: A conceptual framework and model for implementation. *Campus Activities Programming,* 19(9), 56-60.

Mangan, K.S. (1989, April 26). At Texas: An undercurrent of hostility amid efforts to promote multiculturalism. *The Chronicle of Higher Education,* p. A29.

Mann, B.A., and Moser, R.M. (1991). A theoretical model for designing peer initiated activities for racial awareness and appreciation of differences. In J. Dalton (Ed.), *Confronting racial bias in college students.* San Francisco: Jossey-Bass.

Manning, K. (1988). The multi-cultural challenge of the 1990s. *Campus Activities Programming, 21*(3), 44-47.

Muir, D. (1989). White attitudes toward blacks at a deep south university campus, 1963-1968. *Sociology and Social Research, 73*(3), 84-89.

National Institute Against Prejudice and Violence (NIAPV). (1987). *Ethnoviolence on campus: The UMBC study* (Institute Report No. 2). Baltimore: author.

National Institute Against Prejudice and Violence (NIAPV). (1990, June 6). Campus ethnoviolence and the policy options. *The Chronicle of Higher Education,* p. A29.

Shaw, K.A. (1981, November). A shared commitment. A presentation to the University of Wisconsin System Board of Regents.

Stewart, G.M., and Hartt, J.A. (1986). Multiculturalism: A prescription for the college union. *Bulletin of the Association of College Union International, 54*(6), 4-7.

United States Commission on Civil Rights. (1990). *Bigotry and violence on American college campuses.* Washington, D.C.: author.

University of Wisconsin-Madison (1988). *The Madison plan.* Madison: author.

University of Wisconsin-Madison. (1991, January). *The Madison plan three years later.* Madison: author.

University of Wisconsin-Milwaukee. (1990). *The Milwaukee plan.* Milwaukee: author.

University of Wisconsin System (1985). *Minorities in the workplace.* Madison: University of Wisconsin System Board of Regents.

Wehrly, B. (1988, April). Toward a multicultural partnership in higher education. Paper presented at Western Illinois University, Macomb, Illinois. (ERIC Document Reproduction Service No. ED 308 731.)

Wiche Regional Policy Committee on Minorities in Higher Education. (1987). *From minority to majority: Education and the future of the Southwest.* Boulder, Colorado: Western Interstate Commission for Higher Education.

Appendix B

Responses to Campus Racism Survey for Student Leaders

	Agree	*Neutral*	*Disagree*
1. Most students at (name) approve of interracial friendship.	58.2%	27.7%	14.1%
2. Most students at (name) do not approve of interracial dating.	43.2	29.6	27.2
3. You have experienced or been part of a racist incident.	31.3	15.3	53.4
4. Racism does not affect faculty/student or staff/student relationships at (name).	29.5	26.7	43.8
5. Racist comments/jokes are heard often among your college peers.	35.6	22.0	42.4
6. (Name) is not a socially integrated campus.	39.2	27.3	33.0
7. Racism does not exist at (name).	10.2	27.3	62.5
8. You have experienced specific incidents of racism at (name).	21.7	24.5	53.8

	Agree	*Neutral*	*Disagree*
9. Other universities or college campuses are more racist than (name).	25.2%	57.9	17.0
10. Racial prejudice is still very common.	78.7	13.5	7.9
11. You have been physically threatened by someone who is white/black.	16.6	15.4	68.0
12. Most white Americans do not like blacks.	18.6	15.7	65.7
13. Most African Americans do not like whites.	28.4	43.2	28.8
14. Affirmative action programs and policies are effective ways to remedy past racial discrimination practices.	22.2	39.8	38.0
15. Shoal Creek Country Club should have the right to admit members on the basis of race.	33.7	11.7	54.6
16. Multicultural programs are necessary to increase awareness of differences on campus and to retard racism.	75.3	15.8	8.9

	Agree	*Neutral*	*Disagree*
17. Civil rights marches through Forsythe County, Georgia, served to spark racial conflicts across the country.	24.8%	35.7%	39.6%

About the Editors

Melvin C. Terrell is vice president for student affairs and associate professor of counselor education at Northeastern Illinois University. He has served as a student affairs administrator and member of the teaching faculty at other universities. He received his Ph.D. in 1978 from Southern Illinois University in Higher Education Administration, and he participated in postdoctoral study at the Institute of Educational Management, Harvard University, in 1986.

Margaret H. Duggar is the technical editor of the monograph. In addition, she has coauthored several articles with Melvin C. Terrell on student affairs issues. Duggar is a professor of English at Chicago State University. She received her Ph.D. from Indiana University, Bloomington, in 1972. She also served as a Board of Governors Administrative Fellow in the Division of Student Affairs at Northeastern Illinois University in 1989.